Anthropological Thought

Anthropological Thought

Venkata Mohan

Notion Press

Old No. 38, New No. 6
McNichols Road, Chetpet
Chennai - 600 031

First Published by Notion Press 2018
Copyright © Venkata Mohan 2018
All Rights Reserved.

ISBN 978-1-948372-47-3

Marvin Harris

To me, reading Marvin Harris was like a rite of passage to the world of social sciences. His style of critiquing clearly and boldly while offering his own perspective inspired me.

Venkata Mohan

PREFACE

What is culture? How should one study it? Is a science of culture possible? And what is science anyway? Many thinkers have been attempting to answer these questions. This book covers the answers provided by anthropologists ranging from classical evolutionists to postmodernists.

Why Bruce Lee on the cover page? Anthropological Thought is divided in terms of schools; martial arts in terms of styles. Bruce Lee once wanted to develop a perfect school but found that any school has its limitations, and all schools condition man. Thus evolved his philosophy: 'No way as way, No limitation as limitation.' This is what anthropologists should ponder over.

Bruce Lee developed his philosophy after reading J. Krishnamurti. I included Bruce Lee as a way of inviting anthropologists to look at their theories in the light of Krishnamurti's philosophy.

Students of *Anthropological Thought* can also refer to my *Sociological Thought* for certain issues not covered in this book. For more insight, they can read (1) Karl Marx for materialism (2) Emile Durkheim for evolutionism and functionalism (3) R.K. Merton for criticism of functionalism (4) Max Weber for methodology.

I covered postmodernism extensively in *Sociological Thought* which includes the philosophers who inspired postmodernism as well as recent thinkers who are called postmodernists. Students can read (5) Immanuel Kant, Edmund Husserl, Alfred Schutz, Jacques Derrida, Jean Francois Lyotard, Jean Baudrillard and Michel Foucault.

Venkata Mohan

Contents

Part 1

CLASSICAL EVOLUTIONISM

1. E. B. Tylor

E.B. Tylor (1832 – 1917): Despite not having a university degree, Tylor became one of the leading anthropologists in England. It is interesting to know how he became an anthropologist.

Tylor was a businessman's son, who left school at the age of 16 to join his father's firm. Illness, however, forced him to abandon his work. As advised by doctors he spent time in travelling and other leisure activities. His travel was instrumental in his becoming an anthropologist.

He spent a year touring the United States. In Havana, Tylor met Christy, a well-known antiquarian, who encouraged Tylor to accompany him on his visit to Mexico – a land of archeological relics and curious traditions. In 1861, he published his *Anahuac*, an anecdotal travelogue about his Mexican tour. In this book, we can see his interest in Anthropology. Afterwards, he began to write several articles on anthropological topics.

His first substantial anthropological work is *Researches into the Early History of Mankind* (1865). His book *The Primitive*

Culture (1871) was the corner-stone of his career. The theme of this book is evolutionism. His book *Anthropology*, which was a general introduction to the field, was published in 1881.

Definition of culture

"Culture… is that complex whole which includes knowledge, belief, art, morals, law, custom and any other capabilities and habits acquired by man as a member of society." – Tylor.

Pause for a minute and ponder over the definition. What according to you is the single most important word in the definition?

The word "acquired" in the above definition is very significant. This definition emphasizes that culture is learnt and not inherited. Quite importantly we also learn that culture includes many things. It is a complex whole; in fact it is a way of life. Thus culture is a comprehensive concept. His definition is considered the first scientific effort to define culture, which is the central theme of anthropology.

Origins of religions

Visualize the process of death: a living body becoming a dead one in less than a second.

What happens? What is it that left the body?

In dreams, man sees himself meeting known/unknown people, visiting places. Tylor reasoned (conjectured!) that primitive man may have tried to understand this phenomenon through conceptualization of an intangible object called soul.

Tylor even defines soul as "a thin unsubstantial human

image, in its nature a sort of vapor, film or shadow." Thus primitive man may have conceived the 'soul' to explain the puzzling phenomenon of death and dreams. Soul returns after a dream, but after death it fails to return. This was probably the starting-point of religion. Animism (anima means soul) is the "belief in soul or spirits". This is considered the most primitive phase in the evolution of religious thought. Tylor explains how.

Having invented the soul, primitive man realized that the soul was superior to the body because of its greater mobility and durability. He first began to admire the souls of the dead, later started worshipping them, attributing powers to them. Since spirits could also reside in material objects, these would acquire special powers and become fetishes. Eventually, fetishes were given the shape of images, and idolatry was born, elevating the spirits to the rank of gods. Each god controlled a specific aspect of nature or life. This was the stage of polytheism.

Hierarchy among gods is attributed to the prevalent and emerging hierarchy in society. In the hierarchy of gods, one god became a supreme deity. Thus came about monotheism.

That is almost a fictional account. There are not many anthropologists today who think that Tylor is right. There is no proof that the primitive man thought the way Tylor presumed. Moreover, the sole function of religion is not simply to explain some puzzling phenomena. Religion has many social functions. Many anthropologists have criticized Tylor for his exclusive focus on cognitive aspects of religion.

Stages in human progress

Tylor maintained that culture evolved from the simple to the complex, passing through the stages of savagery, barbarism and civilization. But he did not say that all societies would follow the same evolutionary scheme. He conceded that there could be a number of exceptions. (Harris 1968: 172).

He did not perforce equate specific cultures into any of these stages. He did believe, however, that his own culture had reached the stage of civilization. His main interest was to reconstruct the evolution of particular cultural traits or institutions rather than establish overall stages of cultures.

Evolution and progress are central to his theory. He even viewed art in terms of a single evolutionary scale. He spoke of the Egyptian wall paintings as "a style half-way between the lowest and the highest". In spite of their cleverness, the ancient Egyptians "have not quite left behind the savage stage of art". Theirs are "picture-writings rather than pictures". ('Picture-writings' means signs rather than faithful representations.)

Methodology

Tylor used two important methods in the pursuit of his evolutionary doctrine. 1. The comparative method 2. The analysis of survivals.

(1)   Comparative Method: In this method he gathered data relating to the contemporary cultures. He assumed that contemporary simple cultures, more or less, resemble extinct cultures. That is, the culture of some contemporary societies resembles the culture of Paleolithic; the culture of some other groups resembles the culture of Neolithic. The data he collected was used to show the evolutionary trends. For example, in studying firearms, one begins with the early and crude forms of weapons, such as the flint-lock rifle, and moves on to the most modern and sophisticated weapons.

(2) Analysis of Survivals: In all societies ancient patterns of thought and behavior have survived beyond the conditions which gave rise to them, and these patterns serve "as proofs and examples" of an earlier stage of development. For example, why do people say "Krishna" or "Rama" ("God bless you" among the English) after sneezing? To Tylor, it indicated an earlier belief that sneezing was an attempt of the soul to leave the body, and invoking God was to retain the soul. This particular habit is proof of an old belief. Thus "survivals" help in reconstructing the past.

Behind these principles is the assumption that anthropologists can "re-think" the process through which something has come about. Tylor's account of evolution of religion reveals to us that by "re-thinking" Tylor meant that one has to join the minds with the savage to trace cultural evolution. Tylor also emphasizes that one should always take into account the native's level of knowledge in "re-thinking" the institutions.

Contribution

According to Harris, "perhaps the greatest anthropological paper of the 19th century" was Tylor's *On the Method of Investigating the Development of Institutions— Applied to Laws of Marriage and Descent*. Using a sample of about 300 to 400 societies, Tylor invested the comparative method with a statistical basis.

Let us understand his methodology with an example from his paper. Tylor found that there were 45 cases of avoidance between the husband and his wife's relatives, 8 cases of mutual avoidance and 13 cases of avoidance between the wife and her husband's relatives. Later he tabulated patterns of post-marital residence: matrilocality (65), temporary matrilocality giving way

6

to final patrilocality (76) and patrilocality (141). By comparing these two sets of data, he concluded that "the ceremonial avoidance by the husband of the wife's family is in some way connected with his living with them and vice versa as to the wife and the husband's family." He called such probabilities of associations "adhesions". (Today we call them correlations)

Further, Tylor also saw an evolutionary trend from matrilineality and matrilocality into patrilineality and patrilocality. As matrilocality was evolving into patrilocality, there were corresponding changes in the rules of avoidance. However, the negative instances, for example, the cases of patrilocality and avoidance by the husband of his wife's parents, are not explainable.

They were accounted by the concept of "survivals"! The theory of evolution needs to be supported by a theory of survivals, which by itself has no empirical basis. Tylor is considered to be the founder of the modern statistical cross-cultural approach as represented in the work of George P. Murdock and the *Human Relations Area Files*.

Questions to think about

1. How did Tylor become an anthropologist? What are his major works?
2. Explain Tylor's definition of culture.
3. Why is animism considered the origin of religion by Tylor?
4. Is Tylor's approach highly cognitive?
5. What according to Tylor are the stages of culture?
6. What is the role of 'survivals' in the comparative method?
7. What does Tylor mean by re-thinking institutions in the study of culture?
8. What are the 'adhesions' that Tylor found in his study of culture? What do we call them today?

2. L.H. Morgan

Lewis Henry Morgan (1818-81) was born in Aurora, New York. He studied law and settled as a lawyer. All his life he lived in close proximity to Iroquois Indians. Like many Americans, he was attracted to clubs. After graduating from college, he joined a young men's club, the Grand Order of the Iroquois. One day he met a young Seneca Indian by name Ely Parker. He was a law student, spoke fluent English, and brought Morgan in contact with Indian chiefs. When Parker was invited to speak at the Order, he didn't speak about the ancient lore of his tribe, rather he talked about how his people were being driven from their land. Impressed, Morgan took their side and assisted Seneca in their legal battles with the Government. Morgan also observed that the Indian customs were rapidly changing, and that their customs should be recorded before it was too late. Visiting and interviewing many Indians, Morgan collected a great amount of data, and published them in his first book *The League of the Iroquois* (1851). In this book, he described dances, games, religion, language, political organization and family organization of the Iroquois.

One feature of Iroquois that particularly attracted him was their system of addressing their relatives. An Iroquois child called all his mother's sisters "mother", all his father's brothers "father". Morgan called this system "classificatory" and his own "descriptive." He soon discovered that Obijwa Indians, who lived at Marquette, Michigan, too had the classificatory system.

He thought if the classificatory system was found in all American Indians, it would prove the unity of their origin. If the same was found even in Asia, it would prove Asiatic origin of Indians. With this hypothesis, Morgan constructed a questionnaire with 200 questions and with financial aid from the Smithsonian Institution he mailed the questionnaire to distant lands (This was how data used to be gathered before the development of fieldwork traditions). From the responses to the questionnaire he found that his hypothesis of Asiatic origin of American Indians was correct. These findings appeared in his *Systems of Consanguinity and Affinity of the Human Family* (1870). In this he also traced the evolution of the human family from sexual promiscuity to monogamy through fifteen stages of evolution.

But his interpretations were questioned by some. One important question was raised by John Lubbock. Going by Morgan's data, he said since the classificatory system was also present in Australia and Polynesia, how could Morgan prove that only American Indians were of Asiatic origin. Morgan had no answer to this question. It was Joshua McIlvaine, a minister and a Sanskrit scholar, who pointed out to Morgan that widespread occurrence of the classificatory system might not prove common origins but only mean they belonged to an earlier stage of human development.

Morgan began to understand the wider implications of his findings. Meanwhile he read Darwin's *Origin of Species*. He began to work on the reconstruction of the world history rather than that of American Indians only. The result was his most famous *Ancient Society*, subtitled *Researches in the Lines of Human Progress from Savagery through Barbarism to Civilization* (1877).

Evolutionary scheme

In *Ancient Society*, he envisioned human history as consisting of three major "ethnical periods" – Savagery, Barbarism and Civilization. The periods of Savagery and Barbarism are further divided. Each period is characterized by certain advancements.

Savagery
- *Lower*: Invention of speech, subsistence on fruits and nuts (passed out of existence).
- *Middle*: Fishing and the use of fire, e.g. Australians and most Polynesians.
- *Upper*: Bow and arrow.

Barbarism
- *Lower*: Pottery, e.g. Indian tribes east of the Missouri river.
- *Middle*: Domestication of animals in the Old World; cultivation of maize by irrigation, adobe and stone brick buildings in the New World, e.g. village Indians in Mexico, Central America and Peru.
- *Upper*: Iron smelting, use of iron tools, e.g. Homeric Greeks, ancient Italians.

Civilization

- Phonetic alphabet and writing.

He wrote, "Each of these periods has a distinct culture and exhibits a mode of life more or less special and peculiar to itself. This specialization of ethnical periods renders it possible to treat a particular society according to its condition of relative advancement, and to make it a subject of independent study and discussion."

The salient features of his scheme are: 1) Unlike Tylor, Morgan assigned specific known cultures to his various stages. 2) Except for Civilization, Morgan used the criteria of subsistence and material culture for the recognition of the periods.

Moreover, he constructed evolutionary sequences of family organization, kinship terminology, descent patterns, socio-political organization and rules of inheritance of property and fitted them into the scheme of Savagery-Barbarism-Civilization, thus painting a fairly complete picture of human evolution.

Criticism

Morgan did carefully work out his scheme. He tried to answer as to why and how institutions changed. His answers were of a functionalist nature: aspects of socio-political organization were interrelated with one another and were tied to technological developments and economic pursuits, thus making the scheme internally coherent. This shows that Morgan recognized cultures as functional wholes.

But his grand scheme, with its sequences and correlations, has too many errors. Latter-day ethnography disproved many of his correlations. For example, 1) Hawaiians with a kinship system that was early in Morgan's scheme developed agriculture, were highly stratified, and possessed a complex form of government. 2) In the Old World, civilization existed long before the use of iron. 3) The Aztecs who had no knowledge of iron smelting had a state government and developed a system of writing. There are many such examples which disprove his scheme.

The most important reason for many errors in the scheme is his wrong application of the comparative method. He believed that contemporary simple societies in their totality were accurate reflections of the past. Tylor reconstructed evolution of only specific institutions, not whole cultures as Morgan did. That is why many of Morgan's correlations could not stand the scrutiny of latter-day ethnography.

What are the enduring aspects of Morgan's work? Present-day anthropologists have dropped the offensive words of "savagery" and "barbarism" but accepted a general historical sequence of hunting-gathering to domestication of plants and animals to civilization, which is indicated by writing. Morgan is also correct in his observation that kinship-based societies preceded state-based organization; and stratification came increasingly to the fore; and concepts of property were not developed in early times; and it is quite likely that descriptive kinship terminology and monogamy are relatively late in their emergence. Also it is through Morgan's work that anthropologists learnt social significance of kinship terminology.

Morgan and Marx

Marx read *Ancient Society* and found in it a confirmation of his own materialistic conception of history. Shortly before his death, he left instructions for Engels to present Morgan's findings to a wider audience, the result of which was Engels's *The Origin of the Family, Private Property and the State*. This bears the distinct imprint of *The Researches of Lewis Henry Morgan* (1884).

Why was Marx so much impressed? Morgan's stages are characterized by methods of production and tools of production – fishing, fire, bow and arrow, domestication, iron smelting etc., After making them the milestones in the history of human progress, he gave details of corresponding changes in various other sectors of society. To Marx, it clearly threw light on the materialist basis of history. Moreover, since neither Marx nor Engels knew firsthand anything about the primitives, Morgan definitely appeared a specialist.

In retrospect it is recognized that Marx and Engels were only partially justified in making Morgan a historical materialist. Morgan was not concerned with the force behind the change. Sometimes he cited intelligence or knowledge or brain size or the plan of the Supreme Intelligence or God. Confused eclecticism rather than historical materialism was the hallmark of his writings. (Malefijt: 155)

Evolution of family

Morgan began a global inquiry about kinship systems. He sent a questionnaire to consular officials, missionaries and scientists around the world requesting information about kinship terms. He got data from 139 groups drawn from North America, Asia, Oceania and Europe.

After going through the data, Morgan concluded that kinship systems could be divided into two types — descriptive and classificatory. Semitic, Aryan and Uralian families of kinship are following the descriptive. Ganowanian, Turanian and Malayan are following the classificatory.

The Semitic system was found among Arabs, Hebrews and Armenians. The Aryan system was found among the speakers of Persian, Sanskrit and all European languages. Uralian was found among Turk, Magyar, Finn and Estonian populations. Ganowanian was the term used for native Americans. Turian included Chinese, Japanese, Hindu and other groups of the Indian subcontinent. Malayan included Hawaiians, Maoris and all other Oceanic groups. (From this identify the systems relevant to India.)

Morgan does not stop with the classification. He draws a strange conclusion. The line of demarcation between the classificatory and descriptive "gives nearly the line of demarcation between civilized and uncivilized nations[1]."

What is the connection between kinship terminology and civilization? How is a classificatory system correlated with lack of civilization? Morgan linked kinship terms with the type of marriage. He argued that classificatory systems are followed by the societies that did not develop monogamy as the norm.

The Hawaiian kinship system is a case in point. Ego uses the same kin term for father, father's brother and also mother's brother. All male members of the father's generation are given the same term as father. All the female members of the mother's generation are given the same term as mother, In one's generation all are brothers and sisters. In this kinship terminology, only gender and generation are variables.

Morgan wondered how is it that all male members are given one term and all female members another term? To Morgan, the system reflected "promiscuous intercourse within prescribed limits. The existence of this custom necessarily implies an

1 All the quotations are from *Visions of Culture*

antecedent condition of promiscuous intercourse, involving the cohabitation of brothers and sisters, and perhaps of parents and child; thus finding mankind in a condition akin to that of the inferior animals, and more intensely barbarous than we have been accustomed to regard as a possible state of man."

Today's anthropologists would of course completely disagree with that. Ember and Ember explain that Hawaiian terminology tends to be correlated with the presence of large extended families, bilocal residence pattern and absence of unlineal descent groups. That is to say, they are societies where there are no clan-based loyalties, but people live in large families and couple can live either on husband's side or wife's side. That creates conditions where all women of the mother's generation are called 'mother' and all men of the father's generation are called 'father'. This need not suggest any promiscuity either in the present or in the distant past.

To Morgan, all societies went through the same processes. What are descriptive today were at one time classificatory. But why then did a classificatory move towards a descriptive one? Morgan guesses. Communal husbands fought against other men to defend their communal wives. Such fights over a period of time led to one man fighting for only one woman resulting in monogamy. Thus promiscuity evolved into monogamy.

Rise of private property, according to Morgan, reinforced this trend. "There is one powerful motive which might, under certain circumstances, tend to overthrow the classificatory form and the substitution of the descriptive, but it would arise after the attainment of civilization. This is the inheritance of estates. Hence the growth of property and the settlement of its distribution might be expected to lead to a more precise discrimination of consanguinity."

With the "rise of property, the settlement of rights, and above all, with the established certainty of its transmission to lineal descendants" descriptive kin systems evolved. The family "became organized and individualized by property rights and privileges." These ideas were discussed in his *Systems of Consanguinity and Affinity of the Human Family.*

Was there promiscuity at any time?

Morgan was sure that there was at one time promiscuity and societies evolved into monogamous form of marriage. But Ember and Ember argue that marriage – in terms of a stable male-and-female bonding – did not begin with humans at all. It is there in many species of birds and in some mammals including wolves and beavers. So anthropologists asked what factors contribute to the prevalence of marriage.

Investigations reveal that there is one important factor behind marriage: postpartum feeding problem. When females can't simultaneously feed themselves and their babies after birth (postpartum), they tend to have stable matings. Only in those species where there is postpartum feeding problem are stable matings found.

Human females have the same problem. It means marriage – we are referring to monogamous type – was not invented by humans. Humans were born into societies which had marriage! So Morgan's conclusion that humans invented marriage as they progressed would not be correct.

Evolution of government

Morgan discusses in great detail "Growth of the Idea of Government" in *Ancient Society.* What did he mean by government in early societies? He was referring to mechanisms of maintaining social order. At first social control was related to kinship and later to territory. "The experience of mankind … has developed but two plans of government. The first and most ancient was social organization, founded upon gents, phratries and tribes. The second and latest in time was a political organization founded upon territory and property. Under the first a gentile society was created, in which the government dealt with persons through their relation to a genes and tribe. These relations were purely personal. Under the second a political society was created in which the government dealt with persons through their relations to territory, e.g. the township, the country, and the state. These relations were purely territorial. The two plans were fundamentally different. One belongs to ancient society, the other to the modern."

Social control in ancient society was based on kin ties. In the modern world, it is based on political ties. Control moved from kin-based to territory-based. How did this happen? To Morgan, the "gens" (now we call it a lineage) was the "fundamental basis of ancient society." When two or more gentes (the plural form of 'gens') joined they became "phratries" (we call them clans today). When phratries had a single name, spoke a single dialect, an identified territory, then it reached the level of "tribe." When the tribes coalesced, states got formed.

The nature of property also changed along with the type of government. During Savagery, property was buried as grave good when the owner died. During Lower Barbarism, property was distributed among the members of gens when the owner died. During Middle Barbarism, communal ownership of land – with rights to use but not to sell – developed. By the end of Upper Barbarism, state ownership of land as well as individual ownership of land developed. This got well-established during Civilization.

Questions to think about

1. How did Morgan become an anthropologist?
2. Why did Morgan originally believe in Asiatic origin of American Indians? Why did he have to change his opinion?
3. What is Morgan's most important work?
4. Explain the stages of human progress as given by Morgan.
5. How is Morgan's scheme different from Tylor's?
6. What is the contemporary ethnographic evidence of Morgan's classification of human progress?
7. Why was Marx so much impressed by Morgan?
8. Did Morgan believe in historical materialism?
9. What is the most glaring error Morgan committed in understanding kinship terms?
10. What, according to Morgan, was the Aryan system of kinship? Did entire India follow that pattern?
11. Do you think private property played an important role in the evolution of kinship? Does it continue to play it? Explain.
12. How did Morgan explain Hawaiian kinship terminology? How do Ember and Ember explain the same?
13. Do the present anthropologists believe that mankind was at one time promiscuous? What are the views of Ember and Ember?
14. According to Morgan, what is a 'government'? Evaluate his account of evolution of government.

3. James Frazer

"The cycle of *The Golden Bough* depicts, in its sinuous outline, in its play of alternate light and shadow, the long evolution by which the thoughts and efforts of man have passed through the successive stages of Magic, Religion and Science. It is, in some measure, an epic of humanity which, starting from magic, attains to science in its ripe age." – *Frazer*

Sir James Frazer (1854-1941), an English anthropologist, was a great believer in evolutionism. He postulated that every society would pass through three stages – magic, religion and science. Frazer explained that primitive people had a completely wrong notion of natural causes. They believed in magic, which was based on two principles: 1) "law of similarity" and 2) "law of contact". The law of similarity presumed that like produces like. If rain was needed, water was poured out; if an enemy was to be harmed, a doll was fashioned in his image and needles were run through its head. On the other hand, the law of contact presumed that connections remain in force even after separation. One way of harming one's enemy is to get hold of the enemy's nail clippings (or hair) and burn or mutilate them; the same is expected to happen to the enemy. (This may explain why even now our elders insist that we should not carelessly leave nail clippings but collect and throw them out of the house.)

The practitioners of magic soon found out that their laws did not always work. They became helpless and began to lose faith in their ability to control nature. Since they lost faith in manipulating the supernatural powers, they started worshipping them. Thus was born religion.

And the next step was development of science. Science is like magic in the sense that in both cases man was attempting to apply certain laws to control nature. But the difference between science and magic is that science deals with correct laws and magic deals with incorrect laws. Scientific laws are correct because they are based on data which is empirically observable.

Criticism

It would be wrong to say that non-literate people are unscientific. Malinowski's study highlights how the Trobrianders, despite their belief in the efficacy of magic in increasing the productivity of their crops, carry out all the agricultural operations with the rational understanding of cause and effect.

Frazer's theory which claims an evolutionary trend in the change from thought systems dominated by magic, to those by religion and to those by science has no empirical basis. In fact it has been found that magic, religion and science coexist most of the time.

Books written by Frazer include *The Golden Bough* (12 volumes, 1890), *Totemism and Exogamy* (4 volumes, 1910), *The Belief in Immortality and the Worship of the Dead* (3 volumes,

1913-24), *Folklore in the Old Testament* (3 volumes, 1918), and *Aftermath* (a supplement to *The Golden Bough*, 1939).

From the above list it is clear that Frazer was a prolific writer. He was praised for his erudition, his poetic sentiments and for the elegance of his literary style. But he was a very poor theorist. To him facts were more important than theories. He wrote, "It is the fate of theories to be washed away… I hold them chiefly as convenient pegs on which to hang my collection of facts." What he did was to provide a coherent framework for much of the data he had but the framework he formulated was completely unverified.

Questions to think about

1. What is Frazer's most important book?
2. On the connection between magic, religion and science,
    a. What did Frazer say?
    b. What did Malinowski say?
    c. Whom do you support – Frazer or Malinowski and why?
    d. Is there some truth in Frazer's opinion?
3. What is the difference between 'law of contact' and 'law of similarity'?

4. Marvin Harris
on Comparative Method

As all theorists of the latter half of the 19th century used the comparative method, let us discuss the method in more detail. The most important assumption of this method is that socio-cultural systems observable in the present bear differential degrees of resemblance to the extinct cultures. With this assumption, the varieties of contemporary institutions are arranged in a sequence of increasing antiquity assuming that the older forms are the simpler ones.

Using this method, the 19th century evolutionists provided many schemes. While some of them proved decisively that patriarchy came from matriarchy, others proved equally decisively just the reverse. On the basis of the present-day ethnographic evidence, it is clear to us that it would be wrong to make such generalizations. That is why many anthropologists became bitter critics of the evolutionists' schemes and their methods. Lowie and other Boasians felt that "the use of the comparative method was the cardinal error of the evolutionist school." (Harris, 1968: 154).

Marvin Harris disagrees with Lowie's criticism of the comparative method. Harris feels that the comparative method, if applied with adequate caution and care, is a valid method.

"Are there such things as surviving stone-age cultures? The answer, as undeniable today as it was in 1860, is yes." (Harris, 1968:154). By careful application, Harris meant that attention is to be paid to the diversity of cultures and to the various methods of adaptation to ecological conditions. The methodology as such cannot be faulted but its mechanical application has led to many erroneous conclusions.

Of course the effectiveness of the application of the comparative method depends upon how good the ethnographic data of the contemporary simple societies is. There is no doubt that the ethnographic base of the classical evolutionists was grossly inadequate. Careful application also requires the knowledge of how the contemporary simple societies are different from the extinct societies. For example, we can't suppose that contemporary band-organized hunter-gatherers are representatives of the bulk of Paleolithic hunter-gatherers, for the contemporary ones are the refugees driven to unfavorable surroundings.

Let us raise one more question before we conclude our discussion on the comparative method. The question is: what is the relationship between the concepts of survivals and the comparative method? The essence of the concept of survivals is that "phenomena originating under a set of causal conditions of a former era perpetuate themselves into a period during which the original conditions no longer exist." (Harris, 1968:164).

The idea of survivals was used for historical reconstructions. The evolutionists gave different names to this concept, though the idea is the same. Tylor called them "survivals"; Maine called them "legal fictions"; Morgan called them "relics", "traces" or "remains." These survivals are part of the advanced societies though the conditions which led to their origin are no longer present. Survivals thus constituted the proof for the theory of evolution. It is hence not surprising that every classical evolutionist used this concept. That is why Harris felt that "the idea of survivals was an integral part of the comparative method, and that in one form or another it came into use more or less simultaneously in the writings of the great evolutionists."

Questions to think about

According to Marvin Harris,

1. What are the assumptions behind the comparative method?

2. What was wrong with the way the evolutionists used the method?

3. How can this method be used in a better way?

4. How was the concept of survivals important in the comparative method?

Part 2

HISTORICAL PARTICULARISM

5. Franz Boas

Franz Boas (1858-1942) was born and educated in Germany. He first majored in Physics and Mathematics and later shifted to Geography. It was as a geographer that he joined an Arctic expedition to Baffin island in 1883-84. Before the expedition, he was interested in geographical and psychological matters. He thought the discipline he was interested in was "psychophysics". (Harris, 1968: 264) . Before the visit to Baffin island, he believed that geography would determine culture. But his observations on Baffin island and his latter-day studies proved to him that so much of cultural variation is possible under the same geographic conditions. He thus rejected geographical determinism. His shift from geography to ethnography paralleled his rejection of geographic determinism.

When Boas returned to Germany, he started working for the Royal Ethnographic Museum in Berlin. During this time he associated himself with leading anthropologists. Working with the British Columbia collections at the museum and with two Bella Coola Indians in the city, Boas found himself attracted to the Northern Pacific culture. He planned an ethnological expedition which took him to British Columbia in 1886 to begin a study of the region, especially of the Kwakiutl Indians.

As Boas was a Jew having liberal leftist views he found that the social environment in Germany was not congenial to him. Between 1887 and 1896, he received several appointments in New York, Worcester and Chicago, which he accepted. Each of these posts afforded him the opportunity to pursue his anthropological research. In 1896 he began teaching in Columbia University, where he remained until his retirement in 1937.

Boas became the most influential figure of 20th century anthropology. During his career at Colombia University till his death in 1942, he trained a great many famous anthropologists, such as Alfred Kroeber, Alexander Goldenweiser, Robert Lowie, Margaret Mead and Ruth Benedict. He wrote approximately 800 articles, several books and maintained an extensive collection of myths.

Methodological Puritanism

"Unprecedented also was the precise quality of Boas's devotion to the collection of facts. There is a strong puritan element in his outlook. For him, science was very much a sacred enterprise. Those who rushed to conclusions without proper attention to facts were in effect desecrating a temple." – Marvin Harris.

Boas was very cautious in making any generalizations. This cautious approach was very much needed during that period because many anthropologists of his time were prone to making undue generalizations without any factual basis. Let us go through the statements made by some of Boas's contemporaries:

"Just as patriarchy gives way to hierarchy and hierarchy to absolute monarchy, so limited monarchy is giving way to democracy or republicanism; already the foremost nation of the earth is a republic and other civilized nations are either republican or undergoing changes in the direction of republicanism." – William McGee, the first President of the American Anthropological Association.

Does he have any proof that every nation is moving towards republicanism?

Did everyone feel at that time that proof is necessary?

Lester Ward, reviewing a book on the origin of life, wrote: "The book is purely theoretical and no facts are adduced. This is not a criticism of the book. In fact it is one of its beauties. Anyone who reads the book can see that the author's head is full of facts and that all he was trying to do was to reason from a store of facts to certain conclusions. Those who speak disrespectfully of this method are often unable to make any use of their facts, however many they possess."

Lester Ward was no ordinary man; he was one of the founders of American Sociology. He did not think it necessary to substantiate a generalization with facts!

The point is, when many of his contemporaries were busy with fanciful generalizations, Boas set himself the task of investing anthropological research methods and standards of proof with scientific rigor. He felt that facts should precede grand theories.

Critique of Comparative Method

The beginning of the 20th century brought to an end the evolutionists' dominance in cultural anthropology. Its leading opponent was Boas. He pointed out many errors in the use of the comparative method by the evolutionists.

In his article, "Limitations of the Comparative Method of Anthropology" (1896), he said that the major error of the method was its assumption that "the same phenomena are always due to the same causes." Boas argues that this assumption is wrong. Clans, for example, came among the Navaho by the fusion of separate groups, but among the Northwest tribes, they resulted from village fission. Masks are sometimes used as disguises so that harmful spirits will not recognize the person; elsewhere they are worn to frighten off people and spirits and in still other contexts, they are worn to commemorate a deceased relative. So it would be erroneous to consider that the same phenomena are due to the same causes.

"Therefore we must also consider all the ingenious attempts at constructions of a grand system of the evolution of society as of very doubtful value, unless at the same time proof is given that the same phenomena must always have had the same origin. Until this is done, the presumption is always in favor of a variety of courses which historical growth may have taken." – Boas, 1896.

His criticism of evolutionists does not imply that he was an antievolutionist. His paramount interest was not to condemn evolutionism, but to raise standards of scholarship. For example, when he reviewed Leo Frobenus, one of the forerunners of the German diffusionist school, he said: "By following the methods presented in this book, anything and everything can be proved.

It is a fiction, not science." To sum up, he was not against any school, but against premature generalization.

Did Boas believe in the discovery of universal laws? There were so many debates on this point. It is, however, now clear that his own views were constantly changing. In 1886, he said: "The frequent occurrence of similar phenomenon in cultural areas that have no historical contact suggests that important results may be derived from their study, for it shows that the human mind develops everywhere according to the same laws. The discovery of these is the greatest aim of our science." In 1920 he softened his stand. He said, "It is of course true that we can never hope to obtain incontrovertible data relating to the chronological sequence of events, but certain general broad outlines can be ascertained with a high degree of probability, even of certainty." By 1932, he became disillusioned with the discovery of any laws. He said, "The phenomena of our science are so individualized, so exposed to outer accident, that no set of accidents could explain them. It seems to me doubtful whether valid cultural laws can be found."

The change in his tone is in some ways related to the limitations of his research methods.

Historical Particularism: methods and results

It all started with an attempt to introduce rigorous methodology criticizing unwarranted generalizations. Boas's students maintained that their teacher had only trained them to pursue their varied interests, mindful of the data, free of prejudice, and distrustful of all grand schemes. They denied that Boas was the center of any "school". For example, Margaret Mead said, "Characteristically there are no methods named after

Boas, just as there is no Boas school." With the passage of time, however, a definite central theme came to be associated with the Boasian period, which today is called historical particularism. It is called so because of its focus on the histories of particular cultures.

To get an insight into historical particularism, we need to know about the two methods of cognizing reality: deduction and induction. Deduction means making a generalization by logical reasoning or intuition and verifying it later empirically. Induction means observing experimenting and then generalizing. It means facts first, theory later.

Boas followed the method of induction. In the words of Marvin Harris, "Boas was guided by a distinctive sense of inductive purity, which he transmitted to a generation of followers." Harris traces the limitations of Boas methods to his "inductive purity".

Boas rejected many types of generalizations. We have already discussed his objection to the use of the comparative method, where he said that similar phenomena were not due to similar causes, except in very limited geographic areas. So one can't show the similarity of institutions and then generalize on evolutionary trends. He rejected uniformity of the mind as an explanation because man does not obey the same laws everywhere. Similarity of environment was equally ruled out, because it could be shown that different forms of culture existed in similar environments and vice versa.

His approach was to focus on a single area and to study it in detail, collecting as many facts as possible. That is, he called for an investigation of the unique histories of individual cultures. On his part, Boas studied Kwakiutl society. His work was concerned with all aspects of the society. Folk tales, mythology, religion, art, ceremony and technology. He even did considerable work on the food of the natives. In total, he produced about 5000 pages of Kwakiutl ethnography.

The result of collecting facts excessively is that they defied synthesis. Codere, who made the greatest use of Boas's material, said, "It is not possible to present a synthesized account of Kwakiutl culture based upon Boas's works"! The problem was that data was collected without any hypotheses. Crucial things were neglected and many unnecessary things described in detail.

Basic philosophical error

The theme of Boasian research strategy is: Collect facts first, theories will come later. As stated by Radin "The essence of Boas's method was… to gather facts and ever more facts. And permit them to speak for themselves…" This proposal appears quite sensible till we see the logical consequences of such an attitude to research.

How are we to collect facts? We can neither collect nor handle all the facts. It is impossible even for a super computer to handle all the facts about a single grain of sand. And how could we possibly collect or handle all the facts about a society? The normal mode of scientific procedure is to have a hypothesis, collect relevant facts and verify the hypothesis. It means that it is impossible to discover things simply by pure induction; hypothesis is necessary to guide collection of data.

Einstein says, "There is no inductive method which could lead to the fundamental concept of physics. Failure to understand this fact constituted the basic philosophic error of so many investigators of the nineteenth century … We now realize with special clarity, how much in error are those theorists, who believe that theory comes inductively from experience…"

If Einstein had been asked to comment on the Boasian research program, he would have said, "It contained a basic philosophical error."

Questions to think about

1. How did Boas come to reject geographical determinism?

2. Name some anthropologists Boas trained.

3. Why was Boas against the comparative method?

4. Did Boas believe in discovering laws of culture?

5. Why is Boas's method called historical particularism?

6. How is the method of induction different from the method of deduction?

7. Whom did Boas study?

8. What, according to Marvin Harris, is the basic problem with Boas's approach?

Part 3

DIFFUSIONISM

Schools of diffusionism

To the evolutionists, every society passed through certain stages. If there are similarities among societies, it is because they are at the same stage. If there are differences, it is because they are at different stages of evolution. Cultural change was nothing but movement from one stage to another. There is another school by name diffusionism that explains culture in a different way; that is in terms of diffusion and migration.

While diffusion refers to acquiring traits by imitation, migration implies that culture carriers moved away from their original settlements and moved to other parts of the world, taking their cultural inventory with them and adapting them to the new environmental conditions. However, the impression that evolutionists denied diffusion is incorrect. They clearly recognized diffusion and even they felt that cultural traits were more often imitated than invented (Malefijt:160)

There are three schools of diffusionists: British, German-Austrian and the American. The most prominent British diffusionists were W.H.R. Rivers (1864-1922), G. Elliot Smith (1871-1937), William J.Perry (1887-1949).

6. British School

W.H.R.Rivers

Rivers was "the founder of the trend" (Harris, 1968:380). He became a diffusionist toward the end of his life. In his earlier writings like The Toda (1906), Rivers made no excessive diffusionary explanations, though Todas were strongly influenced by Hinduism. He was converted to diffusionism when he was writing *The History of the Melanesian Society* (1914). He began to offer explanations in terms of diffusion which meant that he began to explain the differences and similarities between cultures of Oceania in terms of migrations, additions, losses and mixing of cultural traits.

For example, he found that on some Melanesian islands, people had no canoes. He explained that the use of canoes must have been once prevalent, but may have been lost later perhaps due to the death of canoe craft guilds. He reasoned that people would not have reached their present position without them. In Australia, he noted five different burial rituals, in an otherwise homogeneous population. He attributed this diversity to the advent of small boatloads of migrants, whose presence could not be detected. He reasoned that otherwise this diversity would not be possible, because the aborigines were not inventive. (note the assumption.)

Smith and Perry applied explanations in terms of diffusion on a worldwide scale.

G.Elliot Smith

Smith and Perry stated that most aspects of higher civilization were developed in Egypt and diffused to the rest of the world. Smith visited Egypt once and was impressed by it. Coming back to England, he was struck by the similarities between the Egyptian complex of large stone monuments in association with sun worship and that of English megaliths such as Stone-henge. He thought that primitive Druids could not have invented these structures on their own (note the assumption) and concluded that they must have imitated the Egyptian structures. He later came to know about similar structures the world over. He came to believe that Mayan pyramids, Japanese pagodas, Cambodian temples and American Indian burial mounds were all imitations of Egyptian structures. He thus came to the conclusion that all civilizations originated in Egypt. The details of his theory are...

Before the spread of Egyptian civilization, the earth was inhabited by "Natural Man" who not only lacked domesticated animals, agriculture, houses, clothing, but also religion, social organization, hereditary chiefs and formal laws or ceremonies of marriage or burial. Around 4000 B.C., the inhabitants of the Nile valley saw barley seeds sprouting and began to plant more seeds and slowly developed agriculture. Thenceforth, in rapid succession, they invented pottery, basketry, matting, houses; learned to domesticate animals; built towns; and began to bury their dead in cemeteries and developed notions of deities. As they progressed in civilization, they set about journeying by land and sea in search of precious metals and other raw materials. Thus they rapidly spread, by diffusion and colonization, varieties of the original archaic civilization founded on the banks of the Nile.

If everyone imitated Egypt, why is there so much cultural variation? It is because some prospered, some others degenerated. Many of the new centers of archaic civilization survived and prospered, some, like the New World Maya, declined or died out. Many cultures of contemporary primitive societies represent decline from archaic civilized status rather than advance from the condition of "natural man". Some are a mixture of "natural man" and degenerated cultures; some others a mixture of different varieties of degenerated cultures.

Needless to say, this pan-Egyptian theory has no takers now. It has been completely abandoned.

The books in which he developed his theory are: 1. *The Origin of Civilization* (1928) 2. *The Diffusion of Culture* (1933).

William J. Perry

He did not put forward any independent scheme of diffusion; he simply supported the theory of Elliot Smith and popularized it in his book *The Children of the Sun* (1923).

Criticism of the School

No one denies that there is diffusion; even the evolutionists did not deny this truth. The British school, however, gave too much importance to diffusion. They assumed that man is basically uninventive and as invention is rare, imitation is in the natural order of things. In offering proof of imitation, they did not take into account entirely different functions and cultural meanings of the traits that are said to have been copies. For example, to Smith any structure, even vaguely resembling a pyramid, was the proof of imitation. He did not consider that in Egypt, pyramids are tombs and that similar structures in Cambodia are temples.

To sum up, though present-day anthropologists do consider diffusion as an important source of cultural change, they regard the British diffusionists' view as too extreme to have any basis in fact.

Questions to think about

1. What are the salient features of diffusionism?
2. Who are the prominent anthropologists belonging to
      the British school of diffusionism?
3. When did Rivers become a diffusionist?
4. Is migration a part of diffusionism?
5. Who said all the important aspects of higher civilization
   came from Egypt?
6. How did Smith explain diversity of cultures?
7. Is diffusion an important aspect of cultural change now?
8. Name some books written by British diffusionists.

7. German-Austrian School

This school was inspired by Friedrich Ratzel (1844-1904), Fritz Graebner (1877-1934) and Father Wilhelm Schmidt (1868-1954) laid the foundations of this school. This school has also come to be known as the Kulturkreis or "culture circle" school.

Friedrich Ratzel

He is the founder of anthropogeography – the study of people's relationships with neighboring countries, particularly in terms of trait distributions. Ratzel had criticized his contemporaries, especially Adolf Bastian, for relying too heavily on explanations in terms of psychic unity and independent invention. Ratzel insisted that diffusion should be ruled out, before attributing cross-cultural similarities to independent invention. To him, " It seems far more correct to credit the intellect of 'natural races' with great sterility in all that does not touch the most immediate objects of life."

In every case of diffusion, adaptation to a particular culture involves some changes. Then how can we be sure that something is only a transformed form of the original and not independently invented? It is here that Ratzel gave his principle : the criterion of form. It states that similarities between two cultural elements which do not automatically arise out of the nature, material, or purpose of the traits or objects should be interpreted as resulting from diffusion, regardless of the distance which separates the two instances. A canoe paddle needs a blade, a spear must have a point. Such similarities can't show historical connection. On the other hand, if paddles have similar incised ornamentation or spears have features attached to their shafts, this cannot be accidental but must simply be a result of borrowing or migration. Applying this principle to the history of the African bow and arrow, he noted that the cross-section of the bow shaft, the fastening of the bow strings, and the featuring of the arrows were quite like those in Indonesia and so he concluded that they were borrowed.

(A note: Schmidt attributed the discovery of criterion of form to Ratzel, but in the view of Harris it was first formulated by William Robertson, an 18th century evolutionist. Harris, 1968:384).

Leo Frobenius

He was Ratzel's pupil and took his ideas several steps further. He drew attention to similarities between masks, houses, drums, clothing and shields in Melanesia, Indonesia and West Africa. Thus Frobenius proved that similarities existed not only between single elements of culture, but also between whole culture complexes. He attributed these similarities to migration.

To Ratzel's criterion of form, he added one more principle, "geographical statistics." It states that the probability of historical relationship between two items increases as the number of additional items showing similarities increases, that is, several similarities prove more than a single one. Furthermore, he introduced another factor, namely, the biological or development criterion. According to this, not only similarities, but significant differences related to ecological adaptation could become indicators of historical connections.

Fritz Graebner

Ratzel's criterion of form and Frobenius's geographical statistics were vigorously combined in the strategy of the Kulturkreis school, whose main figures were Graebner and Schmidt. In his *Die Method der Ethnologie* (1911), Graebner discussed the utility of these two principles in tracing diffusionary processes. (Note: Harris explains that the first rule was called the "Criterion of Form" by Graebner, and the "Criterion of Quality" by Schmidt. Both called the second rule the "Criterion of Quantity." Harris, 1968: 384).

Graebner reasoned that the early man invented the basics of culture, such as language and tool-making but soon formed a number of small bands that became isolated. Each of these bands developed its own culture and they were the "primeval cultures", whose members in time spread out in all directions, eventually populating all continents. He thought that the task of ethnology was to reconstruct all these developments. And he did considerable amount of work in this direction. In particular the data he collected is still considered to be useful.

He was also interested in reconstructing the culture-history of regions. Starting with Oceania, Graebner reconstructed six successive cultural developments. The earliest and the most primitive 'Kreis' was Tasmanian, followed by Australian boomerang culture, totemic hunters, two-class horticulturists, Melanesian bow culture, and Polynesian patrilineal culture. Each of these, alone or in combination with other cultures, had counterparts in Africa and elsewhere.

Wilhelm Schmidt

Like Graebner, Schmidt too attempted to reconstruct a limited number of original culture circles. All the world history was thus to be understood as the diffusion of these Kreise out of the regions in which they were supposed to have evolved. Of all the schemes of this school, Schmidt's was the most influential one.

Schmidt distinguished four major phases or grades of culture circles: Primitive, Primary, Secondary and Tertiary. Within each of the grades there were several Kreise.

Primitive:

1. The central or exogamous Kreis, distinguished by their exogamous hordes and their monogamous families, e.g. the pygmy people of Africa and Asia.
2. The Arctic Kreis, exogamous with sexual equality, e.g. Eskimos.
3. The Antarctic Kreis, exogamous with sex totems, e.g. South-eastern Australians, Bushmen.

Primary:

1. Patriarchical cattle-raising nomads.
2. Exogamous patrilineal totemic higher hunters.
3. Exogamous, matrilineal, village-dwelling horticulturists.

Secondary:

Free Patrilineal systems. (Polynesia, India, Southern Europe)	Free matrilineal systems. (Southern China, Melanesia)

Tertiary:

Earliest higher civilization of Asia, Europe and America.

According to Marvin Harris, the most striking feature of this scheme is its evolutionism. The succession of "grades" is like the familiar sequence of "stages" leading from hunting and gathering types of socio-cultural systems through horticultural and pastoral types and on to complex stratified civilizations. Moreover, Schmidt attempted to associate the sequences of grades with the main European archaeological divisions of prehistory, strengthening the evolutionary significance of the scheme.

Schmidt did not merely give a general sequence of transformation from hunting, gathering to civilization; he gave many details of the sequence. For example, he gave details of "classic phase of mother right" and discussed how it disappeared. His reconstructions were like the ones offered by evolutionists. Actually, the only difference between Morgan's and Schmidt's evolutionistic schemes is that Schmidt's main sequence is postulated to have happened only once, whereas aspects of Morgan's sequence were postulated to have happened over and over again.

Even Schmidt adopted the same method which the 19th century evolutionists used – comparative method. The Kreise were not only "circles" but they were "Strata" – a part of a universal chronological scheme, which was based on the assumption that contemporary cultures could be arranged according to the degree of primitiveness.

Criticism:

- His scheme had no empirical basis, and was highly speculative.

- No culture circles could be conclusively established.

- At best the above can give an insight into the spread of some cultural items, but it has   overlooked the reasons behind acceptance, rejection or modifications.

Today the Kulturkreis school is practically defunct and has no adherents.

Questions to think about

1. Which anthropologists come under the German-Austrian school of diffusionism?

2. What is meant by 'criterion of form'? How is this principle used to prove diffusion?

3. What is meant by 'geographical statistics'?

4. What is meant by 'criterion of quality' and 'criterion of quantity'?

5. Who explained the history of culture in terms of 'culture circles'?

8. American School

This was led by Clark Wissler (1870-1947) and Alfred Kroeber (1876 – 1960). Both were students of Boas. This approach is called "culture-area" approach. "The geographical regions that displayed close cultural similarities were called "culture areas", and their similarities were explained by diffusion.

Clark Wissler:

He was dissatisfied with earlier writers who had treated American Indian populations as if they were one. Recognizing their diversity, Wissler went about classifying the societies according to their dominant traits and geographical locations. Taking subsistence as the most basic factor, he arrived at eight food areas.

Subsistence	area
Caribou	Eskimo
Bison	Great Plains
Salmon	North Pacific Coast
Wild seeds	California
Eastern maize	South-east and Eastern Woodland
Intensive agriculture	South-west, Mexico, Peru
Manioc	Amazon region, Caribbean
Guanaco	Guanaco

To show the similarities and differences, he began to list many of their cultural elements. He also found it necessary to posit "a culture center" for each of his culture areas. This centre is the place of early settlement from which the various traits had diffused. Elaborating further on the notion of "culture center" Wissler set forth a "law of diffusion". "anthropological traits tend to diffuse in all directions from their centers of origin." This law is the basis of the "age area" principle: the most widely distributed traits around a center would be the oldest, if the direction of diffusion was always from the center outwards. Needless to say, the age-area principle should be applied with great caution. (Think of an obvious example that disproves the age-area principle.)

Alfred Kroeber

It was Wissler who said, "a culture is not to be comprehended until the list of its traits approaches completeness." Much to Kroeber's credit, an attempt was initiated to define culture areas in terms of comprehensive lists of items. These lists were used to establish coefficients of similarity.

But how many traits are required to "approach completeness"? In the first California trait list, published in 1935, Klimek included 430 items. Two years later, Gifford and Kroeber made a list for the Pomo and two neighboring tribes, counting 1,094 traits. The items mentioned in the lists kept on increasing and they touched 7,663 in the list prepared by Vernon Ray working in the region north and north-east of the California tribes. And there are so many other limitations in this approach. For example, how to define a unit of elements? Even a list of 7000 items may not measure the similarity, if traits utilized were not systematically identified on the same level of detail. Polygyny might count for one trait, while bow and arrow might count for four or five. So the trait list approach was soon abandoned.

Though the trait list approach was abandoned, efforts to classify culture areas continued. Kroeber revised Wissler's original division and eventually mapped 7 "grand areas", 21 "areas" and 63 "sub-areas" for North and Central America (1939). Stout recognized 11 areas in South America in 1938, which were narrowed down to 3 by Bennett and Bird in 1949, but increased again to 24 by Murdock in 1951. That there was no consensus on what constituted a culture area and the constant reworking reveals the inherent problems in the concept of culture area.

Thus the culture-area approach had faced many limitations. Steward identified three problems in this approach:

1. Center and boundary may change with passage of time.

2. Culture within the area may change so that it resembles cultures in different areas at different times.

3. A portion of the area may be regarded as containing radically different cultures despite sharing of many features. Actually all these problems were well   illustrated in the case of Kroeber's Greater Southwest Area.

Marvin Harris says the entire concept of diffusion is "sterile." (Harris, 1968:377). According to him, by definition, diffusion can't account for independent invention. Even when we assume that inventions are rare, there is no simple relationship between distance and cultural type; there is deferential receptivity to cultural influences independent of distance. We should explain why a trait has been accepted or rejected, and also show how and why the trait has been modified, if there are modifications. But diffusionists did not pursue such a line of inquiry at all.

Questions to think about

1. Which anthropologists come under the American school of diffusionism?
2. What is the culture-area approach?
3. What is meant by the age-area principle?
4. How is the culture-area approach linked to listing of traits?
5. What are the problems with the culture-area approach?

Part 4

FUNCTIONALISM & STRUCTURAL FUNCTIONALISM

9. Bronislaw Malinowski

"Science is the worst nuisance and the greatest calamity of our days. It has made us into robots, into standardized interchangeable parts of an enormous mechanism. Anthropology, to me at least, was a romantic escape from our over-standardized culture." – Malinowski.

Bronislaw Malinowski (1884-1942) was born in Cracow, Poland. He received his Ph.D. in Physics and Mathematics. Due to his illness, he couldn't pursue research in those subjects. During his sickness he read Frazer's *Golden Bough* which drew him towards anthropology. "No sooner had I begun to read this great work, than I became immersed in it and enslaved by it," he wrote.

He first went to the University of Leipzig and worked under Wundt, an experimental psychologist. In 1910, he went to England, where anthropology was better established. He studied at the London School of Economics under Seligman and Westermarck and conducted library research on the Australian aborigines. In 1913, he became a lecturer at the London School of Economics in the Department of Sociology.

He left England for fieldwork in Australia in 1914. He accompanied other anthropologists who were travelling to Melbourne to attend a meeting convened by the British Association of Anthropologists. No sooner had the scientists gathered than World War I broke out. It was an embarrassing situation for the German and Austrian scholars who all of a sudden were treated as enemy aliens. Some of them were interned for the duration of the war. However, they were given complete freedom to continue working. Malinowski was one among those interned, for he was treated as an Austrian subject (the city of Cracow was then a part of the Austrian Empire).

Throughout World War I, he was allowed to pursue his research. He spent the first six months studying the inhabitants of Mailu, a small island located off the southeast coast of New Guinea. He then shifted his base to the Trobriand Islands, located about 100 miles northeast of New Guinea. He spent about 26 months with the Trobrianders. By this he set new standards in fieldwork: no anthropologist before him had spent that much time in a simple society.

He came back to England in 1920, took a position at the London School of Economics. He was teaching in London till 1938, touring various places around the world. World War II broke out when he was in the US and he stayed there till his death.

Malinowski is considered one of the most important figures of British anthropology. Some of his books are: *Argonauts of the Western Pacific* (1922), *Crime and Custom in Savage Society* (1926), *Sex and Repression in Savage Society* (1927) and *A Scientific Theory of Culture* (1944, published posthumously).

Fieldwork

The most important contribution of Malinowski is not his theory of functionalism, but his methodology of fieldwork. He set new standards in fieldwork. He stayed among primitives studying them longer than anyone had before him. For the first time, research was conducted in the native language. He initiated the method of participant observation.

He paid attention to every detail of daily life. He described the routine of a man's working day: the care he took of his body, his personal ambitions, passing friendships as well as the tone of conversations, the laughing and weeping, thus conveying to the reader a sense of the actuality of Trobriand life.

He faced many problems during his fieldwork. There were times when he felt depressed and times when he faced health problems – real or imaginary. At times he felt hostile towards the natives. To escape from his frustrations he read novels. In the beginning, he spent only a part of his time with the natives. However, later he deliberately cut his contacts with whites and put up a tent among the natives. He poked his nose into everything and they soon regarded him "as part and parcel of their life, a necessary evil or nuisance."

He used his diary as an emotional outlet. In 1967, long after his death, Malinowski's widow gave his diaries for publication. The diary revealed the problems of fieldwork and of adjustment to long periods of isolation in alien surroundings. These diaries provided seminal ideas in latter-day construction of research methodologies.

Theory of Functionalism

Malinowski is regarded as one of the founders of functionalism in anthropology. However, the term "functionalism" has many different meanings in his work. According to Elvin Hatch (From *Theories of Man and Culture*, 1973) Malinowski, in his works, employed three different modes of interpretations, all of them could be stretched to fit 'functionalism'. Those three types are: 1. Integrationalism, 2. The dualistic form of utilitarianism, 3. The monistic form of utilitarianism. Of these three, the monistic form is most important because when Malinowski began to elaborate his theoretical orientation he moved in this direction. Also, it is this type that is "fully compatible with the other parts of Malinowski's scheme" and so "it constitutes the chief feature of his functional approach". (Hatch: 335). We will study the third form in detail but briefly peruse the first two.

a) Integrationalism

It means that all elements of culture are interrelated and so a change in any element of culture necessarily affects others. In *Argonauts of the Western Pacific*, though the 'kula system' forms the central theme, it has been presented by tracing the interconnections with the other aspects of the Trobriand culture, such as gardening, magic, canoe-building and chiefship. This is an example of integrationalism in his functionalism. Similarly, in a monograph *The Sexual Life of Savages*, he focuses on sexual behavior but he relates it to divorce, marriage, chiefship, matriliny etc. This integrationalism enabled Malinowski to present coherent monographs, relating one trait to another, rather than disjointed lists of cultural traits.

b) Dualistic form of Utilitarianism

It means that each aspect of culture is conceived as contributing to the persistence and integrity of society as a whole. Let us discuss this with an example. In the Trobriand society the relations between the clans Malasi and Lukuba are guided and stabilized by a myth. According to the Trobriand myth, people originally lived beneath the surface of the earth and emerged on the surface only a few generations ago. Prior to the emergence, the Lukuba clan, whose totem was dog, held the highest rank. But after the emergence, the Malasi clan, whose totem was pig, became the highest clan. The transformation in the clan hierarchy is explained by the story that when a dog came out it ate the fruit of the noku plant, which is considered dirty. For this supposedly abominable act the dog was reproached by one and all, including the pig, and was thereafter condemned to a lower status. This myth, according to Malinowski, "settles once for all the relations between the two rival clans". Thus he shows how myth serves to legitimize the patterns of social organization and customs in general. In explanations like these, Malinowski's approach is "not at all unlike the approach employed by Radcliffe-Brown". (Hatch: 330) (Do you know of any Indian myth explaining the origin of the caste system? What functions does the myth serve?)

c) Monistic form of Utilitarianism

This views culture, in the words of Malinowski, as "essentially an instrumental apparatus by which man is put in a position to better cope with the concrete specific problems that face him in his environment in the course of the satisfaction of his needs."

Here he has conceptualized culture as an instrument serving man's biological and psychological needs. For example, he found that Trobriand Islanders made extensive use of magic – in the form of spells, charms and potions. He explained that magic functions to reduce the tension and anxieties which result from the uncertainties of life. He found that the islanders used magic when they were fishing in the dangerous open seas but not when they were fishing in calm lagoons. Lagoon-fishing apparently involved no particular dangers and hence provoked no feelings of anxiety. But the uncertainties of open-sea-fishing created tensions that required to be released through magic. Thus, according to Malinowski, magic symbolizes the triumph of hope over fear.

At a more abstract level, he developed a general scheme within which his particular analysis of magic, religion, myth etc. would fit. The central element of this scheme is his notion of institution. According to him culture may be conceived either as a single institution or as a related system of institutions. An institution is "an organized system of purposeful activities." The following are examples of institutions: a tribe, or nation; a clan, which is not a mere category of people but which has a body of common affairs; a household; a group, which is engaged in magic or religious rites; a university; a firm or business.(Hatch:322)

In Malinowski's scheme the importance of the institutions is evidenced from the fact that he decreed (ordered!) that every aspect of culture has to be understood by placing it within the context of its institutional setting.

Each institution has six aspects:

1. the charter, which is a set of values, myths or beliefs which legitimize the activity;
2. the people, who engage in the pursuit;
3. the norms which the group follows;

4. the material apparatus which is employed;

5. the activities themselves;

6. the function of the institution.

Malinowski emphasized that institutions exist to satisfy the needs of the people.

Malinowski contends that there is an immediate and fundamental relationship between the functions of an institution and the needs of human beings. He gave a list of biological needs and the cultural responses to satisfy those needs. His list:

Basic need	Cultural response
Nutrition	Commissariat (food supplies)
Reproduction	Marriage and family
Bodily comfort	Domicile and dress
Safety	Protection and defense
Relaxation	System of play and response
Movement	Activities and system of communication
Growth	Training and apprenticeship

Thus he showed that a great many activities were related to the satisfaction of biological and psychological needs. But not all needs are biological or psychological. For the satisfaction of the basic (bio-psychological) needs culture creates its own needs. These are called "derived needs".

Derived need	Cultural response
Renewal of cultural apparatus	Economics
Charter of behavior and other sanctions	Social control
	Education
Renewal of personnel	Political organization
Organization of force and competition	

Furthermore, each culture has "integrative needs", which are met in part by religious beliefs, magic, systems of knowledge, norms and language. Thus institutions and culture function to satisfy various types of needs.

Criticism

What is the significance of the scheme? One can choose an institution and see what functions it serves or choose a need and study what institutions serve the need. It does not give a holistic insight about culture. That is why Elvin Hatch says, "Malinowski's attempt to bring the institution into direct relationship with biological needs may be the most unfortunate aspect of his work, for he was able to do no more with this scheme than offer such platitudes as the notion that the family functions to promote the health and security of the child. It was an embarrassing failure and yet it became one of the well-known features of his thought. It might have attracted attention away from some of the more enduring ideas which his writing contains." (Hatch: 324).

In summary, the major inadequacies in his theory include:

a) It does not explain why there is cultural variation. Given that the needs of individuals are the same everywhere, why

10. What are the problems with Malinowski's functionalism?
11. How did Malinowski get the idea of participant observation as a research method?
12. What problems did Malinowski face during his stay with the natives?
13. Did Malinowski's attitude regarding the natives and his own culture change? How did that influence his theory?
14. Should his diary be regarded as an important work in anthropology? Explain. Why did he not publish it during his lifetime?

10. Radcliffe-Brown

A.R. Radcliffe-Brown (1881-1955) was born in England. He took his degree in 1904 and promptly became the first anthropology student of W.H.R. Rivers at Cambridge. He did fieldwork among the Andamanese from 1906 to 1908 and among the Australian aborigines from 1910 to 1912.

He worked in various capacities in England, South Africa, Australia, China, Brazil and the USA. He is considered to be one of the most important figures in British Anthropology. He trained a whole generation of anthropologists. Notable among them were Evans-Pritchard, Meyer Fortes, Fred Eggan and Sol Tax.

Malinowski and Radcliffe-Brown

Malinowski and Radcliffe-Brown were contemporaries belonging to the British school of social anthropology. Their perception of anthropological thought was similar to the extent that both rejected classical evolutionism because it was based on hypotheses which were highly conjectural. Similarly, diffusionism did not find favor with them because it did not pay

Bathonga must have passed through a matriarchal phase. Radcliffe-Brown offered an alternative explanation which is synchronic and has no reference to history(i.e. it avoids an evolutionary perspective). His explanation is as follows:

Among the patrilineal Bathonga, since father is a stern patriarch, so will be his brothers and sisters; since mother is a warm and indulgent figure, so will be her brothers and sisters. And also, generally speaking, greatest degree of familiarity is possible only between people of the same sex. Hence, if mother and her sisters are indulgent, then her brother (called malume, which means "male mother" will be even more so. Conversely, if father demands respect, father's sister (called nanani, which means "female father") should be even more aloof. And this is indeed the case.

Structural functional significance of the Bathonga joking relationship is its contribution to the maintenance of the patrilineage.

On socio-cultural laws

Radcliffe-Brown believed that by focusing on social structure, one can arrive at sociocultural laws. Radcliffe-Brown said, "Now with ethnology with its strictly historical method can only tell us that certain things have happened, or have probably or possibly happened, social anthropology with its inductive generalization can tell us how and why things happen, i.e., according to what laws."

In this regard, he opposed the Boasian view that no socio-cultural laws can be found. Radcliffe-Brown attacked the Boasian view in unequivocal terms." I have found it impossible to know what they mean or on what sort of evidence (rational or empirical) they would base their contention. Generalizations about any sort of subject matter are of two kinds: the generalizations of common opinion, and generalizations that have been verified or demonstrated by a systematic examination of evidence afforded by precise observations systematically made. Generalizations of the latter kind are called scientific laws. Those who hold that there are no laws of human society can't hold that there are no generalizations about human society because they themselves hold such generalizations and even make new ones of their own."

What are the socio-cultural laws that structural functionalists found out? To understand the nature of these laws, let us see some of them.

Radcliffe-Brown identified three principles of the classificatory kinship terminology:

- The unity of the sibling group: Brothers and sisters share a feeling of solidarity and are treated as a unit by outsiders. Mother's sister is also addressed as mother.

- The unity of the lineage group: Like siblings, lineage members show solidarity and are treated as a single unit by outsiders.

- The 'generation principle': There is a certain distance or tension between members of succeeding generations, and members of alternating generations tend to share easy and friendly relationships.

Principles like these were regarded as useful for analysis of both kinship terminology and social structure.

He also gave three other sociological laws. "If we could define any universal condition to which a social system would

have to conform, we would thereby have a sociological law…
One such law or necessary condition of continued existence is
that of a certain degree of functional consistency amongst the
constituent parts of the social systems…To this law we may add
a second…rights and duties need to be defined in such a way
that conflict of rights can be resolved without destroying the
structure. Another sociological law is the necessity not merely
for stability, definiteness and consistency in the social structure,
but also for continuity." (Do you think they are really "laws"?)

Criticism

About socio-cultural laws

These so called "laws" are not laws in the conventional
sense. They merely provide some kind of interpretation to
the observed social phenomena. They can't really explain or
predict social phenomena. "The tragedy of Radcliffe-Brown's
contribution to theory is that the 'laws' which he produced
were distinguished by their weakness, their low capacity for
prediction and retrodiction and their vapidity." (Harris, 524).

Radcliffe-Brown himself became aware of the explanatory
impotence of his laws. In his 1935 paper on patrilineal and
matrilineal succession, while showing how all societies must
somehow or other handle the question of lineality in conformity
with the laws of consistency, control of conflict and continuity,
Radcliffe-Brown wrote, "It might be expected that such a paper
as this would deal with the question of what factors determine
the selection by some people of the matrilineal and by others
of the patrilineal principle in determining status or succession.
My opinion is that our knowledge and understanding are
not sufficient to permit us to deal with this problem in any
satisfactory manner."

This admission of inadequacy was repeated in 1941 for the entire field of kinship terminology, one of the lifelong foci of his search for lawful principles. He wrote, "If you ask the question: 'How is it that Omaha (or any tribe we have considered) have the system they do?', then it is obvious that the method of structural analysis does not afford an answer."

Thus it is clear that the laws of structural-functionalism failed to answer important questions. The laws only offer some kind of weak interpretation. According to Marvin Harris, this is not surprising because of two reasons:

1. Techno-economic parameters are not given sufficient place in the scheme of structural-functionalism. Without considering these parameters, science of culture is not possible. He means that social structure shouldn't be the first priority of analysis at all.

2. No diachronic inquiry took place till the 1950's. They "did not take advantage of reputable or otherwise useful historical sources even when these were available in great abundance." (Harris: 526).

About functionalism in general

Functionalisms of both Malinowski and Radcliffe-Brown have certain common limitations. The former looks at the social phenomena and explains how they satisfy individual needs; the latter looks at the same and explains how they contribute to functional unity. Both view societies as if they were well-oiled machines; their various parts working harmoniously. But how far is such a view correct? Certain traits may be neutral in terms of maintenance of the system or some may be even detrimental to society.

Merton believes that early functionalists have made some questionable assumptions. 1) They assumed integration of social system, whereas, according to Merton, it is something to be empirically determined and measured. 2) They assumed that every social item must make positive contributions to the integration of social system. Merton thinks that some items can have negative consequences. 3) Merton also thinks that a researcher has to investigate what can be alternatives to a particular social item why they are not chosen. (From Turner, *The Structure of Sociological Theory.*)

Both Malinowski and Radcliffe-Brown were present-oriented, neglecting historical factors. They only saw the role of a trait as of now, and not how it came about.

Their theoretical orientation, by its very nature, fails to explain cultural variation. Why should individual needs be satisfied only in this way and not in any other way? Why should structure be maintained only by this custom and not by some other one? As Marvin Harris points out, perhaps technological, economical, and ecological factors might have to be considered to answer such questions; but functionalists did not pursue such a line of inquiry at all.

Questions to think about

1. Under whom did Radcliffe-Brown take training? Whom did he train?
2. Where did Radcliffe-Brown conduct his fieldwork?
3. What are the similarities between Malinowski and Radcliffe-Brown?
4. What are the differences between Malinowski and Radcliffe-Brown?
5. What is Durkheim's influence on Radcliffe-Brown?
6. To Radcliffe-Brown, what is social structure? Why is his school called structural functionalism?
7. What are Radcliffe-Brown's views on the possibility of discovering socio-cultural laws?
8. What are the limitations of functionalism in general – of both Malinowski and Radcliffe-Brown – in understanding culture?
9. How has Durkheim influenced the functionalists?
10. What is functional unity?
11. What, according to Radcliffe-Brown, is a social structure?
12. How is a social system more than social structure?
13. What type of groups come under social structure?
14. What is meant by structural functionalism? Examine Marvin Harris's criticism of Radcliffe Brown's approach to the study of society.
15. Give the gist of R.K. Merton's critique of functionalism.
16. Explain the terms 'status' and 'role' occurring in Radcliffe-Brown's structural functionalism.
17. Are cross-cousin marriages part of social structure? Is untouchability a part of it?
18. Is Radcliffe-Brown a cultural materialist?

Part 5

CULTURE & PERSONALITY

11. Ruth Benedict

"Cultures from this point of view are individual psychology thrown large upon the screen, given gigantic proportions and a long time span." – Ruth Benedict.

In the 1920s, some American anthropologists began to study the relationship between culture and personality. The writings of Freud had great influence on this school of thought.

Ruth Fulton Benedict (1887-1948) was a student of Boas. She accepted his view that cultures are discrete entities and integrated wholes, and her friendship with Margaret Mead made her aware of the close relationships between personality and culture. These two concepts together made her think in terms of culture and the personality of its members. The result was her most famous book, *Patterns of Culture* (1934).

Culture is an integrated whole. A "pattern" is a specific way in which integration takes place; consistent within itself and with the overall temperament of its participants.

To demonstrate this, she compared three societies. The societies and their patterns of culture are given below.

The Zuni of south-western United States

She called the 'Zuni way of life' an 'Apollonian pattern.' Zunis are a very cooperative people; a typical Zuni would rather blend into a group than try to stand out as a superior. This basic pattern manifests itself in many other aspects of their culture. Initiation ceremonies are conducted in a group setting and are never an ordeal. Marriage is relatively simple/ casual. Leadership was either declined or accepted with reluctance. Special positions of power were delegated on a group basis. For example, there is medicine society, rather than a single powerful medicine man. Death calls for little mourning.

The Kwakiutl of western Canada

She described the 'Kwakiutl way of life' as the 'Dionysian pattern'. People are ambitious and striving; and individuality is emphasized in every aspect of life. In the initiation ceremonies, a boy is expected to go out by himself and experience a personal relationship with the supernatural. Marriage is not a casual affair as in the case of Zuni, but calls for great celebration. Leadership is characterized by intense struggle for power. The Shaman and priest wielded a lot of power. Death is an occasion for much mourning.

The Debuans of Melanesia

Their culture is magic-ridden, with everyone fearing and hating everyone else. She called their way of life paranoid.

A pattern only describes a typical member of society and in no way assumes that there are no individual differences. To sum up, her point of view is that cultures are integrated, they have patterns, and that these patterns can be conceived in terms of typical personality types.

Criticism

Though many agreed that the tendencies she described were present, they felt that she got such clear personality types only because she de-emphasized and neglected non-conforming data. For example, there are known cases of factional internecine strife among Zunis; also their initiation ceremonies are not as peaceful as was depicted by Benedict. Same is the case with Kwakiutl; quite contrary to what has been depicted they are generally humble in their behavior.

The criticism does not rest merely on the premise that she has been inaccurate in the description of culture. It is more fundamental in nature as it raises an important issue of individual differences and individual adaptations to culture. Are not the individual differences sufficiently large that it becomes difficult to describe any culture in terms of a typical personality?

Questions to think about

1. What is Benedict's view of culture?
2. What cultures did she study? What pattern did she find in them?
3. Does a culture produce a personality?
4. How does *Patterns of Culture* argue cultural relativism?
5. How does it take deviance?
6. How does it take the relationship between the unit and the whole?
7. How does it see the conflict between the individual and society?
8. What is meant by 'pattern of a culture"? According to Ruth Benedict, how is a pattern generated?

12. Margaret Mead

Margaret Mead (1901-78) was a student of Franz Boas. Though she was the first student of Ruth Benedict, as far as her career in anthropology was concerned, she was a contemporary of Benedict because she began her anthropological work in the same year when Benedict got her Ph.D.

Coming of Age in Samoa (1928) was her first major work. It dealt with the question of whether the rebellion that marked adolescent personality in Western cultures was a product of the biological changes at puberty or a result of cultural conditioning. She found that the whole cultural mood in Samoa was much less emotional than that in America. Facts of birth, death and sex were not hidden from Samoan children. Premarital sex was considered natural. Adolescents were not confronted with the necessity of selecting from a variety of often conflicting standards of ethics and values. Adolescence was not marked by stress. Thus, Mead wrote that "the girls' minds were perplexed by no conflicts, troubled by no philosophical queries, beset by no remote ambitions." It means that causes for the stress that adolescents experience in western civilization are more cultural than biological.

Criticism: Like Benedict, Mead has been criticized for the exaggerated nature of her findings. She does not take up the cases of girls whose minds are in conflict; she just treats them as deviants.

In another important work of hers, *Sex and Temperament in Three Primitive Societies,* Mead chose to study the variations in the sex roles. She chose Arapesh, Mundugumor and Tchambuli as the cultures to do fieldwork. She wrote, "In one [Arapesh] both men and women act as we expect women to act – in a mild parental responsive way; in the second [Mundugumor], both act as we expect men to act – in a fierce initiating fashion; and in the third [Tchambuli], the men act according to our stereotype for women – catty, wear curls and go shopping, while the women are energetic, managerial, unadorned partners."

Criticism: Do such categorical generalizations stand the test of empirical verification? The problem with both Benedict and Mead is that in the process of attempting to show a pattern in culture they paid inadequate attention to individual variations. Actually, there is so much of variation even in simple societies that we can't really study cultures without proper statistical validation techniques. But neither Benedict nor Mead used such techniques. Thus their accounts are basically impressionistic.

The limitations of non-quantitative approaches become even more glaring as we go from simple societies to complex ones. In complex societies, the psychic patterns may vary depending upon class, caste or even occupation.

B. Kaplan, after conducting Rorschach tests in four cultures – Zuni, Navaho, Spanish American and Mormon – found that there was so much of variability within each culture. As Kaplan notes, "that great variability exists does not argue against the influence of culture on personality; it means merely that cultural influences do not necessarily create uniformity in a group."

Controversy over her first book

Time magazine listed Margaret Mead as one of the 20th century's 100 most influential scientists and thinkers. It described her as the world's "foremost woman anthropologist." How did she become so famous?

Mead's *Coming of Age in Samoa* (1928) made her famous. She was only in her 20s when she wrote the book. After her fieldwork, instead of submitting her thesis for the academic world, she wrote a book for the general public, which became a big hit. Why were Americans interested in Samoa? They were not. They were interested only in themselves. The book had some provocative things to say about American beliefs.

Mead wrote that the stress that adolescents in America face was not biologically determined as had then been assumed, but shaped by culture. Originally Franz Boas had believed it, he sent Mead to study this phenomenon in a remote culture. Mead went to study the influence of culture on adolescents. Mead found in the stress-free adolescent Samoan culture the proof for the idea that culture was responsible for the stress.

Mead wrote about many things in terms of how Samoa was different. "The Samoan background which makes growing up so easy, so simple a matter, is the general casualness of the whole society. For Samoa is a place where no one plays for very high stakes, no one pays very heavy prices, no one suffers for his convictions or fights to the death for special ends. Disagreements between parent and child are settled by the child's moving across the street, between a man and his village by the man's removal to the next village, between a husband and wife's seducer by a few fine mats… And in personal relations, caring is slight. Love and hate, jealousy and revenge, sorrow and bereavement, are all matters of weeks. From the first months of its life, when a child is handed carelessly from one woman's hands to another's, the lesson is learned of not caring for one person greatly, not setting high hopes on any one relationship[1]."

But what struck the readers was the Samoan attitude towards sex: of the 30 postpubescent girls Mead studied, 17 had heterosexual relations, 22 homosexual relations and some both. Abortions may end pregnancies, although no great fuss is made over 'illegitimate' children and they are incorporated into the household.

Her book proved that a less restrictive life is both possible and desirable. Malinowski only showed how the savages were like us, but Mead showed how in certain ways they might be better. Though Mead wrote many more books and articles later, she was always linked to her work on Samoa. Her later works too emphasised the role of socialization in personality formation, sexual division of labour etc.

Her work questioned

But in 1983, five years after her death, came a book *Margaret Mead and Samoa: The making and Unmaking of an Anthropological Myth*[2] by Derek Freeman (1916-2001), a professional anthropologist. He wrote that he had been

---

1 From *Visions of Culture*

2 Details of this controversy are taken from Clint Talbott's article *Sex, lies and videotape* in Colorado Arts & Sciences magazine (2009).

convinced of Mead's argument, developed interest in Samoans, went to study them and found Mead had been wrong.

His book was based on his fieldwork in 1940s and 1960s. He found the society to be devoutly Christian, patriarchal, violent and sexually inhibited. The society valued virginity so much that there was a custom of having a ceremonial virgin, named taupou, whose chastity the entire village zealously guarded – a custom Mead did not even mention.

Freeman stated that Mead was too young to understand things and unfamiliar with the local language, and more important, she went there with a predetermined notion regarding the role of culture and therefore her work lacked objectivity.

At first it looked as though Freeman had exposed Mead. But as more people closely examined his work they found he was not being fair and honest. In 1983, American Anthropological Association denounced his book as "poorly written, unscientific, irresponsible and misleading."

Freeman did not give up. He went to Samoa again and accidentally met a woman – her name Fa'apua, she was a taupou – who had been Mead's informant and came out with yet another book with more evidence damning Mead, *The Fateful Hoaxing of Margaret Mead: A Historical Analysis of her Samoan Research* (1987). In that book Freeman said, according to Mead's informant, the girls were all lying and joking with Mead about their sex lives which Mead took seriously!

How different versions

After reading Freeman's first book, some came to the conclusion that both the anthropologists might be looking at the society with different theoretical orientations, with different methods and with some time lag.

Mead got her data from 1925. Freeman from 1940s and 1960s. Mead got her data from adolescent girls. Freeman from elderly males; some were even chiefs. Freeman became so close to them that he was even given an honorary title, which touched him. More importantly, society had changed in the intervening period. During Mead's time, though Christianity was there, Mead did not pay much attention to it. Over the years, it might have played a very important role in changing the sexual attitudes. And the way both looked at the custom of taupou also was different. To Freeman that was very important; to Mead it was not.

Conclusions of Paul Shankman

Paul Shankman did fieldwork in Samoa first in 1966 and since then has visited it periodically. He studied this controversy in detail and came up with a book *The Trashing of Margaret Mead: Anatomy of an Anthropological Controversy* (2009). He concludes, "*Coming of Age in Samoa* did include errors of fact and questionable interpretations, as well as overstatements. Mead could have been a more scientific ethnographer of Samoan adolescence. However, Freeman used his knowledge not merely to correct the ethnographic record but to damage Mead's reputation in a deliberate and personal manner."

Shankman came to such a damning conclusion on the basis of Freeman's archives after his death! Some of the things Fa'apua' had said in the unreleased transcripts of 1987 and 1993 interviews were ambiguous and some of the things were clearly incorrect. Freeman knew this, but gave the world a different picture to prove that Mead was wrong. He purposefully glorified the importance of taupou, which in the first place was confined to upper layers of the society, to undermine Mead's reputation.

My evaluation

1)   Does this debate prove the case for postmodernism? It need not. The lack of scientific vigour from Mead's side and sheer dishonesty from Freeman's side showed more objectivity was both possible and desirable.

2)   What is stress-free from a distance can look different when seen closely. Mead found Samoa stress-free, compared to the stress levels in the American society. If that gives the impression that an entire society or a section of the society leads a completely stress-free life and one wants to see what it is like, one is bound to be disappointed. Conflict, stress and sorrow are part and parcel of life.

3)   If one wants to prove how exaggerated Mead's work can be or wants to show how biology plays a significant role, her *Sex and Temperament in Three Primitive Societies*, where she argued that gender socialisation is entirely cultural, is probably more vulnerable to criticism. Freeman didn't try it.

Questions to think about

1. What is Mead's major work? What is the main thesis of that book?
2. How did Mead show that gender roles are culture-specific?
3. How is Mead's work evaluated today?
4. What was provocative about Mead's Coming of Age in Samoa?
5. What do you know about Derek Freeman's criticism of Mead's work?
6. Whom do you support between Mead and Freeman?
7. What is Paul Shankman's take on the controversy over Mead's work?

13. Abram Kardiner

Abram Kardiner (1891-1981) was neo-Freudian, which means that he accepted certain aspects of Freud's theory and modified or rejected certain other aspects. Kardiner believed that the early years of one's life were most crucial in the formation of personality. He later dropped his 'earlier emphasis' on the Oedipus complex and the sexual determinants of culture.

Freud's' original scheme could not be applied to cultural analysis. The familiarity of many anthropologists with the diversity in cultural institutions made them develop serious objections to Freud's scheme. Kardiner however "operated with the barest remnants of Freud's original scheme" (Harris: 435), paying attention to cultural diversity.

The data on which he based his theory was provided by anthropologists. He organized seminars; participants were Sapir, Ruth Benedict, Ruth Bunzel, Ralph Linton, and Cora DuBois.

They contributed ethnographic data to Kardiner's psycho-cultural analysis.

He postulated the existence of a "basic personality structure" typical of a society. He then divided the institutions of any society into two categories – primary and secondary. Primary institutions are responsible for forming the basic personality structure. These institutions are concerned with disciplining, gratifying and inhibiting the deviant tendencies of infant and young children. Secondary institutions are those which "satisfy the needs and tensions created by the primary and fixed ones." Among the secondary institutions, Kardiner gave greatest importance to "taboo systems, religion, rituals, folk tales and techniques of thinking". According to the scheme, primary institutions formed the basic personality structure; and this was projected in the secondary institutions.

If primary institutions changed, the basic personality structure would change and there would be corresponding changes in the secondary institutions. For example, if the economy demanded that the mothers spend much time away from their children, the children might develop feelings of ambiguity towards their mothers and these feelings would be reflected in myths and religious beliefs.

The significance of this scheme is that it attempts to explain magico-religious phenomena by linking it to basic personality structure and primary institutions. In this sense, the contribution of Kardiner is significant given the fact that the magico-religious phenomena always baffled many anthropologists. For example, Morgan wrote, "all primitive religions are grotesque and to some extent unintelligible."

Criticism

The problem with all the neo-Freudian psychocultural analyses is that the linking up of childhood patterns with adult character and cultural forms can be achieved in many alternate ways. (Harris : 440) And here there is so much of scope for speculation.

A major defect in the scheme is that it can't explain the existence of primary institutions as such. Kardiner himself put this problem thus: "… psychology can cast no light whatsoever without the aid of history on how these primary institutions took their final forms. So far as we know, no satisfactory explanations have ever been made of primary institutions."

Questions to think about

1. Why is Kardiner's approach called neo-Freudian?
2. What are primary institutions in a society? What is their role?
3. What are secondary institutions in a society? What is their role?
4. What is the link between the primary institutions and secondary institutions?

14. Cora DuBois

Alice Cora DuBois (1903-91), a member of Kardiner's seminar, carried out fieldwork in a village on the Indonesian island of Alor. She recorded not only traditional ethnographic facts but also collected eight lengthy biographies, dreams and children's drawings and administered a number of projective tests.

Upon her return, she submitted the life histories to Kardiner, the test results to Emile Oberholzer and children's drawings to Trude Schmidl-Waehner for their analysis. They worked 'blind' i.e., without knowledge of the ethnographic data and without consulting one another. The result showed a great deal of correspondence. All noted the shallowness of Alorese emotional life-insecurity, apathy and suspiciousness. These conclusions were made by pooling all individual responses to the various tests and averaging them so that the resulting "psychogram" described the most prevalent personality features of the group. DuBois called this the "modal personality", because it was directly derived from testing, while Kardiner's "basic" personality was inferred from cultural data.

National Character studies

The idea of relating childhood experiences to adult personality and to cultural institutions was applied not only in the case of simple societies, but also in the case of modern nations. There are two such famous instances. These are the attempts to study national character in the neo-Freudian approach.

During the height of the Second World War, Geoffrey Gorer invoked a toilet-training hypothesis to account for "….contrast between the all-pervasive gentleness of Japanese life in Japan, which has charmed nearly every visitor and the overwhelming brutality and sadism of the Japanese at war." According to Gorer, this brutality was associated with "severe early cleanliness training" which created a repressed rage in Japanese infants because they are obliged to control their sphincters before the appropriate muscular and intellectual development has been acquired.

The theory was proposed without the benefit of any fieldwork. After the war, when the hypothesis was put to test it was found to be wrong. Studies by Edward and Margaret Nobeck (1956) and similar other studies showed that Japanese children were not subjected to any severe toilet-training. Moreover, after the war, there was change in the image of the Japanese which had emphasized their brutality.

Russians swaddle their infants during the first year after birth. (Swaddling involves wrapping cloth strips around an infant's body to keep the arms and legs immobile.) According to Gorer and Rickman's study, the infant would experience rage while swaddled, and freedom when swaddling bandages were removed. And this would lead to a kind of manic-depressive adult personality.

These conclusions were reached using indirect research methods. When researches were able to get firsthand data using more representative samples, Gorer's swaddling theory was found to be wrong. It was also found that there is much variation in the central personality modes of the peasants and workers and that of the governing clique.

In other words, it is now clear that early studies of national character were crude attempts to use methods of social sciences to substantiate subjective generalizations about personality differences between complex societies.

While retaining the interest in the relation between child training and adult personality, some anthropologists began to investigate the possible determinants of child-training practices. For example, Herbert Barry, Irvin Child and Margaret Bacon suggested that in agricultural and herding societies, adherence to routine is encouraged while in fishing and hunting societies individual initiative is encouraged. It is because, they reasoned, in the former, mistakes may affect a year's food supply and in the latter, mistakes will affect only the daily food supply. They have found cross-cultural evidence supporting this hypothesis.

One trend is to find out what determines child-training practices. Another important trend is to account for cross-cultural associations between one cultural pattern and another, which is somewhat like an elaboration of Kardiner's ideas. As we discussed earlier, Kardiner linked primary institutions with secondary institutions taking basic personality as the intermediary. Some anthropologists used this strategy. For example, John Whiting and Irvin Child explained that severe punishment for aggression in childhood (a cultural characteristic) may lead to an exaggerated preoccupation with aggression in adulthood (a psychological characteristic), which may in turn predispose adults to believe that aggressive behaviour causes illness (a cultural characteristic).

Questions to think about

1. What is the theme of Cora DuBois's study?
2. What is meant by modal personality?
3. Name the studies made on linking child-rearing practices with adult personality.

15. Ralph Linton

Does a caste produce a specific personality? Does a class produce it? If yes, how does it do it? If no, how will it fail? What is the nature of interaction between culture and personality? Ralph Linton (1893-1953), an American anthropologist, attempts to answer these things in a way that deserves our consideration.

Linton thinks of personality at two levels: central organization and superficial organization. Central organization is something that is deeper to an individual. It consists of invariant aspects, such as degree of introversion/extroversion and other temperaments. Superficial organization is based on the goals and interests of an individual.

What is the relationship between the central organization and the superficial organization? The superficial incorporates the central. Where is culture in this? The superficial is almost determined by the culture in which one is raised. So essentially Linton is conceiving personality in terms of three levels: central, superficial, and cultural. Here superficial does not mean temporary nor does it mean insignificant. It only means at surface level – as an intermediary layer.

What is culture in the context of personality? This refers to the external world as experienced by the person. His caste or class would surely impact his experience with the external world. So personality represents adjustment and integration of one's temperaments with what one faces from outside.

No one, including a rebel, is free from this. Even his rebellion is within a range of acceptability, which is influenced by his culture. No one is free from this enculturation, that is, internalization of culture by an individual. In this sense, even the central is influenced by the culture. Thus Linton looked at personality as consisting of three layers.

In this context Linton coined a term status personality in his book *The Cultural Background of Personality* (1945) to refer to a person whose core is very different from the way his status requires him. If you are a police officer who thinks more about the systemic causes of violence and do not believe in punishing individuals but nevertheless do what you are supposed to do as a police officer, then you are a status personality. Husband and wife may be living in harmony maintaining their status personalities – both playing their roles as expected of them even if their behaviour is against their nature.

Questions to think about

1. What is the difference between central organisation and superficial organisation?
2. How, according to Linton, does personality consist of three layers?
3. What is meant by status personality? What is its significance?
4. How does Linton link personality with culture?

Part 6

STRUCTURALISM

16. L'evi-Strauss

"Ethnology is first of all psychology." – L'evi-Strauss

French structuralism is the most influential anthropological strategy in contemporary Western Europe. This is the strategy that hundreds of trained academic minds in Europe and Americas have found worthy of lifelong study. But this is also the strategy that many anthropologists find unscientific.

The "structure" in structuralism refers exclusively to the mental structures. According to L'evi-Strauss, ethnology is the study of psychological superstructure of socio-cultural systems. To L'evi-Strauss, social phenomena are nothing but objectivated systems of ideas, and that the mind has to be their ultimate explanation. Thus structuralism is a kind of 'psychologic" and it is aimed at discovering basic mental processes and structures.

The structures are "molds" in the mind. In their most elementary form, they are present in all human minds and are ultimately part of the neurophysiology of the human brain. However, each culture fills the "molds" with its own distinctive content. It is the task of structural analysis to show how the surface content in its distinctive way actually expresses or conforms to the underlying universal structures.

Actually this type of thinking was influenced by Emile Durkheim's idea of conscience collective. This collective consciousness or collective conscience is a set of ideas exterior to any given individual but endowed with coercive force over individual thought and behavior. Structuralism is an attempt to explain the conscience collective in terms of a pan-human, neurological-based unconscious mental dialectic.

Structuralism holds that underneath apparently disparate thoughts, there are similar meanings. These hidden meanings are always reducible to two ideas, one of which is the opposite of the other. These pairs of opposed ideas are called binary oppositions. Structures consist of these binary oppositions. Structuralist explanation consists essentially in finding the binary oppositions in the collective social mind. Some commonly identified oppositions are me: other, life: death, culture : nature.

These binary oppositions are sometimes regarded as contradictions which tend to produce third elements as "mediators" or resolutions. The same binary oppositions and their mediators are the same for all cultures and in all ages. (For now the concepts of binary oppositions, mediators, may appear vague, however examples to be discussed later will make them clear.)

The Elementary Structures of Kinship

"Thus it is always the system of exchange that we find at the origin of rules of marriage."- L'evi-Strauss.

L'evi-Strauss had first attracted the attention of the

international anthropological community with his theories about types of kinship and modes of marriage. His book *The Elementary Structures of Kinship* remains an essential starting-point for comparative studies of kinship studies. It organizes and minutely analyses a vast range of phenomena.

L'evi-Strauss takes different systems of kinship and marriage and shows that all forms of marriage and kinship are merely expressions of exchange, in which groups of men bestow women as gifts upon other groups of men who reciprocate. How did he conclude that marriages everywhere are nothing but exchanges of women? His conclusion rests on his hypothesis that the mental structures of all people in all the cultures are the same. And what are the mental structures relevant here?

There is a binary opposition between "mine" and "yours" or between "us" and "them". The mediator in this opposition is a gift and the best of all mediators is the gift of women. All varieties of kinship are nothing but manifestations of this fundamental facet of the mind. To repeat, all varieties of kinship and marriage can be looked at as systems of exchange of women; and the exchange is nothing but a gift, and the gift functions as a mechanism to resolve the binary opposition between "us" and "them". Thus the central theme of his book is that all varieties of kinship and marriage systems are best understood as manifestations of the binary oppositions between mine and yours or "us" and "them."

Criticism of Marvin Harris

It is questionable whether in every society, marriage can be looked upon as a system of exchange of women. Many (paleo-technic) Paleolithic hunter-gatherers have bilateral, ambilineal and ambilocal organizations in which group membership is too fluid, for the notion of exchange to apply.

According to L'evi-Strauss, one understands a kinship system when it is reduced to a particular type of exchange; and one understands exchange when it is seen as a way of resolving the binary opposition between "mine" and "yours".

But exchange is not the only way of resolving this opposition; sharing women, i.e., sexual communism, is another way through which the binary opposition may be resolved. It hence becomes relevant for us to ask as to why societies have not adopted this solution to overcome the binary opposition.

The accepted reason today which explains avoidance of this type of sexual communism – or incest – is not that 'we have mental structures against incest' but that which postulates that incest involves certain adverse biological and social consequences.

Restricted and generalized exchange

According to L'evi-Strauss, there are two forms of marital exchange: 1. restricted exchange 2. generalised exchange

In the first type, if a man from say, group A, marries a woman from say, group B, then a man from group B must be able to marry a woman from group A. It means that the groups involved can exchange women in both directions, i.e., A ← B and B ← A are possible. (arrow indicates the direction in which the women are given.)

In the 2nd type, if a man from group A marries a woman from group B, then a man from group B cannot marry a woman from group A, but must marry a woman from a third group,

C. A← B, B← C, C ← A are possible and many more groups (D, E, F etc.,) can be involved in this cycle. The point however to be noted is that in this type of exchange women are always given in a unidirectional way.

According to L'evi-Strauss, not only restricted exchange but generalized exchange too is an example of reciprocity. The difference between restricted exchange and generalized exchange is that, in restricted exchange both groups give to and take from each other, whereas in generalized exchange a group gives women to one group and takes from some other group. Thus generalized exchange involves a "cycle" of flow of women; the cycle becomes possible because of the return flow of women.

In restricted exchange, a man can marry his mother's brother's daughter or his father's sister's daughter. This is the symmetrical form of cross-cousin marriage. In generalized exchange, cross-cousin marriage is asymmetrical, that is either patrilateral or matrilateral. L'evi-Strauss showed that patrilateral cross-cousin marriage is not a mirror image of the matrilateral one. In the matrilateral one, the cycle A →B →C→A is true of all generations. But in the patrilateral one, it is A →B→C→A in one generation and A← B ← C ←A in the next generation. This leads to shunting effect, and so while long cycles are associated with the matrilateral type, short cycles are associated with the patrilateral type. (Draw the diagrams of the matrilateral type and the patrilateral type to check the veracity of the above.)

Though both forms of asymmetrical marriage are relatively uncommon, the matrilateral variety occurs much more frequently than the patrilateral. Explaining the above empirical fact L'evi-Strauss says that long cycles, associated with the matrilateral type, are more common because they "favor better integration of the group". Let us read through his own words.

"What is meant by this? Instead of constituting an overall system… Marriage with the father's sister's daughter is incapable of attaining a form other than that of a multitude of small closed systems, juxtaposed one to the other, without ever being able to realize an overall structure. If, then in the final analysis, marriage with the father's sister's daughter is less frequent than that with the mother's brother's daughter, it is because the latter not only permits but favors a better integration of the group."

It is this explanation that generated a lot of controversy.

Criticism

No societies have been found in which matrilateral marriage can be said to "realize an overall structure". Although cycles like A → B →C→ A do occur, they rarely involve every member of the community. Instead, there are several such cycles. The best empirical example of long cycles – those found among the Purum of Eastern Manipur – have many short cycles and many instances of direct exchange. Actually there was a lot of controversy about the interpretation of the Purum case. But now it is clear that the Purum case finally helped to reveal absence of empirical basis to Structuralists' explanations. (Harris 1979: 177).

The raw and the cooked

"The boiled can most often be ascribed to what might be called an 'endo cuisine,' prepared for domestic use, destined to a small closed group, while the roasted belongs to 'exocuisine", that which one offers to guests. Formerly in France, boiled chicken was for the family meal, whole roasted meat was for the banquet." - L'evi-Strauss

Structuralism is not confined to analysis of kinship only. L'evi-Strauss was struck by the idea that meals have a structure. All cultures unconsciously send out messages coded in the medium of foods and in the modes of preparation of the foods. The basic contrasts in this culinary language are those between cooked, raw and rotted foods. Within the category of cooked foods, the main structural components communicate messages about whether the product is on the side of nature or on the side of culture. Boiled food is on the cultural side, because boiling requires a container and a barrier of water between the food and the fire. Roasted food is on the side of nature, because roasting brings food and flame into direct contact. Hence the formula: Roasted: boiled:: nature : culture

With this formula, he explains that roasted food is served to guests, because guests are associated with nature, whereas boiled food is served to close kin, because they are at the center of cultural life. (What do you say about this formula? Is it applicable to our culture?)

L'evi-Strauss does not stop there; with this formula he makes a prediction about practices of cannibals. Sometimes cannibalism involves eating enemy strangers, and at other times it involves eating one's own relatives. According to his prediction, since kin are associated with culture, they should be boiled; and since strangers are associated with nature, they should be roasted. Well, the mental structures discussed by L'evi-Strauss may never be verified, but predictions about cooking habits of cannibals can definitely be verified. Let us see the results.

Criticism

Paul Shankaman (1969) tested these predictions. He found that in a sample of 60 cannibal societies, 17 boiled, 20 roasted, and 6 did both. Of the 60 societies, 29 were exo-cannibals, and 26 endo-cannibals, 5 were both exo- and endo-cannibals. Did the exo-cannibals do more of roasting as the theory predicts? No, 34% of both the groups were roasters. Did endo-cannibals do more of boiling? No, on the contrary, over half of the exos were boilers while only two of the endos were boilers. Shankaman also found that in those societies that were using only one method, neither roasting nor boiling was the most common method of cooking. Instead they followed a method not at all considered by L'evi-Strauss – namely, baking. It is also found that 1/3rd of societies prepare any person, be he a relative or stranger, in more than one way. Moreover, it is also found that different groups in the same society follow different methods.

In setting forth a defense of the raw, the cooked and the rotted, Edmund Leach admits that some readers "might begin to suspect that the whole argument was an elaborate joke."

If not a joke, what else? Aren't the structuralists taking us for a ride?

The case of the tricky coyote

According to L'evi-Strauss, "Mythical thought always progresses from the awareness of opposites towards their resolution." These mediators or resolutions are then likely to be transformed into new binary dialectical contrasts, which in turn produce new mediators. To explain why North American Indian myths personify the supernatural tricksters as a coyote, (small wolf, living in North America) or a raven, L'evi-Strauss sets up an opposition between agriculture and warfare as an analogy of the opposition between life and death (agriculture sustains life, war leads to death).

agriculture: warfare :: life : death

The mediator between the binary oppositions of agriculture and warfare is said to be hunting (because hunting is life-sustaining war against animals). Agriculture is associated with plants while hunting animals and eating are associated with beasts of prey. This leads to a new opposition: herbivores: beasts of prey. The mediator of this opposition is a scavenger-type animal that does not kill what it eats, viz. a coyote or a raven. Thus raven or coyote mediate life and death, do good and evil at the same time, and hence are sometimes cunning but at other times victims of circumstances.

Criticism

He gave a very big explanation of why a supernatural trickster is personified as a coyote. It is felt that the explanation is unnecessary because of the simple reason that coyote is in reality an extremely cunning animal. It is considered one of the most difficult of animals to catch or trap. Coyotes frequently follow along behind larger carnivores, waiting for a chance to steal a portion of the catch. For example, when a bear catches an animal, they dart in to nip the bear in the leg, and then dart off with the prey when the startled bear lets it fall. The tricky nature of the coyote has in fact been given in biological nomenclature itself. (Canis latrans frustrior – Tricky coyote).

Thus if supernatural trickster is personified as coyote, it is because coyote is a trickster. L'evi-Strauss has missed this simple point, and instead given lengthy explanations.

My evaluation

I am giving Marvin Harris's account (taken from *Cultural Materialism*). It definitely appears one-sided. But I would like to tell you that I have not blindly accepted Harris's account. I know where exactly I don't agree with Harris. I was willing to walk an extra mile to see the truth in L'evi-Strauss theory. Firstly, while Harris was particular that any theory should be able to explain differences and similarities, I would be content if a theory explains only similarities. This is because I know explaining similarities is not an easy thing and it can also be very insightful; J. Krishnamurti always showed the similarities among the individuals in a very insightful way and pointed out to the oneness of human experience.

Secondly, Harris wants empirical evidence for everything. I am not that bothered about evidence. I agree with the Structuralist's point that a theory may not be concerned with empirical proof but with "understanding". I know, again from J. Krishnamurti, that there may be certain things that are difficult to prove but they do definitely enhance our understanding of ourselves or society. I am also aware that the central point of Freud, that is 'the role of the unconscious', is really helpful in explaining things, but does not do very well in any tests calling for empirical evidence. So it is my conviction that there is always a possibility of a trade-off between profundity and empirical evidence. Things that are really profound may be difficult to prove. Those which are easy to prove may not be really profound. If L'evi-Strauss can postulate things that are really profound, I am willing to concede a lot of ground on proof.

Thus I read Structuralism, making many allowances. But I must confess that the whole thing turned out to be a big disappointment. Now I am certain that structuralism as practiced by L'evi-Strauss cannot lead us to where we want to go in the quest of knowledge. It is after considerable deliberation that I have chosen to agree with Marvin Harris's point that "there is distinct possibility that structuralists' structures exist only in the imaginations of the structuralists themselves." (Harris, 1979:177).

I came to conclude that the fundamental approach of structuralists – of finding the binary oppositions in the collective social mind – is a futile attempt.

Major works of L'evi-Strauss

Claud L'evi-Strauss (1908-2009) was born in Brussels to French parents and spent his childhood and youth in Paris. He first studied law and philosophy and thereafter was attracted to anthropology. He made many field trips to central Brazil. He worked in Brazil, France and the USA in various capacities. His major books are:

- The Elementary Structures of Kinship, 1949.
- Structural Anthropology, 1958.
- Totemism, 1962.
- Savage Mind, 1962.
- Mythologiques (Four volumes, 1964, 1966, 1968, 1972)
- An Introduction to the Science of Mythology, 1973.

Irawati Karve on kinship in India

Irawati Karve, in an article *Kinship Map of India,* discusses kinship rules with some materialist explanations. There is huge diversity in India – in terms of region, caste, language, ethnicity. But here we are discussing only a broad trend. She contrasts the North Indian system with that in South India. In North

India, the kin groups aimed to expand, recruit new groups. She explains the rules of alliance with that end.

For example, (1) the four-clan rule followed in North India says a man can't marry a woman of his clan, his mother's clan, father's mother's clan and mother's mother's clan. This means that the man has to find somebody distant. This is an example of kin group aiming expansion. (2) Man should marry someone outside one's village or neighbouring places. This rule is local exogamy, which also reinforces expansion.

Both North India and South India follow patrilocal and patrilineal systems. Irawati Karve also explains the North Indian system in terms of reinforcement of patriarchy. In some castes, there are clans which are hierarchically arranged. In such cases, (3) hypergamy is followed in mate selection: a man from a higher clan marries a woman from a lower clan. Its reverse, the hypogamy, is not allowed. The boy-giving clan should be superior to the girl-giving clan. This rule reinforces gender domination. (4) Irawati Karve mentions that even villages are arranged hierarchically. The boy-giving village is considered superior to the girl-giving village. A boy-giving village can't give its girl to its girl-giving village. So the saying goes, 'man from the west, girl from the east.' It means women move only in one direction and not in both directions. If women are moving only in one direction, it is easier to dominate them. This reinforces patriarchy.

The South Indian system is different. One big difference is that cross-cousin marriages are preferred. What does this mean? Alliance rules prefer consolidation of relations with the already related, instead of going for alliances with new groups. Cross-cousin marriages also dent patriarchy, because a woman is going to live with in-laws who are already closely related.

Irawati Karve makes some interesting observations on the types of cross-cousin marriages. No cross-cousin marriage is permitted in the North. Both matri-cross and patri-cross cousin marriages are permitted in the South. In Central India, some castes pick up matri-cross and not patri-cross. How can one explain this?

Matri-cross and patri-cross are not mirror images of each other. In a patrilineal and patrilocal society, matri-cross and patri-cross have different implications. In a patri-cross, women flow in both directions across groups. When women flow in both directions, the groups can't be hierarchically arranged. In matri-cross, women flow only in one direction which means groups can be hierarchically arranged. So, certain castes in Central India pick up matri-cross through which they can preserve hierarchical arrangement with other groups, though by accepting patri-cross they undermine patriarchy.

Irawati Karve shows that rules of alliance can be explained in terms of 1) whether kin groups want to expand or consolidate, 2) whether they want to generate hierarchical relations across groups or not and 3) whether they want to strengthen patriarchy or not. And one can attempt to explain why the groups want what they want.

On the issue of expansion vs consolidation, Irawati Karve thinks that North Indians wanted to expand because of their pastoralist traditions and South Indians did not have pastoralist traditions. This is very much a materialist explanation.

Thus kinship-related questions can be answered without resorting to mental structures. When L'evi-Strauss shows how a particular rule does a better job in integrating the whole society, he can explain in terms of materialist causes why the society gave high priority to integration. This is to say, long cycles or short cycles can be explained without reference to mental structures. Where is the need for structuralism?

Questions to think about

1. What are the 'structures' L'evi-Strauss refers to?
2. What is Durkheim's influence on L'evi-Strauss?
3. What are binary opposites? What are mediators?
4. What is the theme of The Elementary Structures of Kinship?
5. How is generalized exchange of women different from restricted exchange?
6. Show how patrilineal cross-cousin marriage is not a mirror image of matrilineal cross-cousin marriage.
7. What is a long cycle and a short cycle in the context of the L'evi-Strauss theory of kinship?
8. How did L'evi-Strauss explain various methods of cooking? Evaluate his explanation.
9. How did L'evi-Strauss explain coyote being considered tricky? Evaluate his explanation.
10. Is there a collective unconscious? If so, where is it?
11. Is there a collective social mind?
12. How reasonable is the idea that marriage is an expression of relationship between groups?
13. What is a symmetric form of cross-cousin marriage?
14. Are patri-cross-cousin marriages possible between groups with hierarchical difference? Explain.
15. Can't we think in terms of women as gifts without positing mental structures?

16. Can't we think in terms of the integrative needs of a society without positing mental structures?
17. How does Irawati Karve explain the differences between kinship system of North India and that of South India?
18. Don't Irawati Karve's explanations show that structuralism is not needed to explain kinship?

17. Edmund Leach

Edmund Leach (1910-89) is the most important British exponent of L'evi-Strauss's structuralism.

Marvin Harris examines his explanation of traffic signals.

"With traffic lights on both railways and roads, green means go and red means stop…if we want to devise a further signal with an intermediate meaning we choose the color yellow. We do this because, in the spectrum, it lies midway between green and red… the color system and the signal system have the same structure; the one is a transformation of the other." – Leach.

Leach feels that the mind dichotomizes the spectrum – make a binary opposition out of a continuum. It will use the extremes to build that opposition and the logical centre to mediate those extremes. Thus the railroad and road signal system is a "transformation" of the universal color code, which is an expression of the structure of the mind.

Criticism: Frederick Gamst (1975) has shown that Leach's example is full of errors. All traffic signal systems have a common point of origin in the 19th century England. Gamst analyzed the history of the signal system. He found that in the history of development of traffic signals, many colors, including white, black and blue, were used and experimented with. And also there is variation of the signal system from place to place and from time to time. He finally showed that the modern traffic signal system evolved in conjunction with a series of technical achievements in the fields of color technology, glass and electric illumination and not as a result of any underlying structural processes.

Questions to think about

1. How did Edmund Leach explain traffic signals? Evaluate his explanation.

consumption are not merely technological processes; they are social processes as well."

But don't other subsystems influence the technological system? White agrees that they do and this is how: "This is not to say, of course, that social systems do not condition the operation of technologies or that social and technological systems are not affected by ideologies. They do and are. But to condition is one thing; to determine, quite another."

The view 'that the technological factor is the determinant of a cultural system' makes White a cultural materialist. A materialist is one who opposes the view that 'ideas determine culture and its evolution' – the view held by an *Idealist*. While Hegel believed that ideas shape social change, Marx believed that material forces shape social change. Hegel's theory is called *Idealism*, and Marx's is called *Materialism*.

White gives an interesting example of how notions of female beauty (an ideology) are shaped by the technological system. "In cultures where technological control over food supply is slight and food is frequently scarce as a consequence, a fat woman is often regarded as beautiful. In cultures where food is abundant and women work little, obesity is likely to be regarded as unsightful." Surely size zero would not be an ideal in a scarce society!

After proposing that the technological system is the determinant of a culture system, White goes into the specifics of that technology. He proposes one variable that measures technological advancement – energy. The first stage is invention of tools. The second stage is Neolithic Revolution. The third stage is use of fossil fuels. Thus White divides human history in terms of energy use from tool-making to Industrial Revolution.

White thinks there is this fourth stage which involves the use of atomic energy. We know now that he was not right about the fourth. Atomic energy did not bring energy revolution.

He links cultural evolution to energy evolution. "The degree of cultural development, measured in terms of amount of the human need-serving goods and services produced per capita, is determined by the amount of energy harnessed per capita and by the efficiency of the technological means with which it is put to work. We express this concisely and succinctly with the following formula: $E \times T \rightarrow C$, in which C represents the degree of cultural development, E the amount of energy harnessed per capita per year, and T the quality of efficiency of the tools employed in the expenditure of energy. We can now formulate the basic law of cultural evolution: Other factors remaining constant, culture evolves as the amount of energy harnessed per capita per year is increased, or as the efficiency of the instrumental means of putting the energy to work is increased. Both factors may increase simultaneously of course."

So energy evolves, and with it culture. But what precisely is culture to White? "The functions of culture are to relate man to his environment – his terrestrial habitat and the circumambient cosmos – on the one hand, and to relate man to man on the other." So culture is functional. It relates man to man and his habitat. That relationship becomes more efficient as one progresses. The core source of that increased efficiency is evolution in the form of energy.

23. Victor Turner

Victor Turner (1920-83) was a British symbolic anthropologist. He was trained under the school that believed in studying the processes by which social cohesion that Durkheim referred to is being attained. Turner was guided by Gluckman, who asked him to study the Ndembu tribe in Africa. The trend at that time was to discover concrete institutions and formal relations that were contributing to organic solidarity. But Turner developed a different theoretical orientation.

Turner did not reject the idea of social cohesion. He only found that it was interesting to study social cohesion through the study of symbols. What is a symbol? By itself it does not mean anything. But to the natives, it stands for something of the culture, which an anthropologist has to decipher. A tri-colour piece of cloth with a particular colour combination represents India; it has emotional significance to Indians. But to others it is just a piece of cloth. Symbol stands for something. It has to be interpreted from the viewpoint of the native. Sacred thread that twice-born varnas wear is a symbol, it is not just a thread worn casually.

Turner was particularly interested in the rites of passage. To him, the symbolism associated with these rites revealed a lot about the Ndembu society. In the analysis of these rites, Turner took the classification first made by Arnold van Gannep (1873-1957) who divided the rites of passage into three stages: preliminal, liminal and postliminal. Limen, in Latin, meant 'threshold'.

What is a rite of passage? It is a rite marking transition from one stage in life to another stage in life. For example, puberty function marks transition from girl to woman. What is expected of a woman is different from what is expected of a girl. She has to behave differently and the people around her have to treat her differently. The stage of transition is called 'liminal', the stage before is preliminal and the one after is postliminal. As a girl she had a pattern to follow, as a woman she had a pattern to follow. During the transition, she did not fit into the patterns of either a girl or a woman. Rites of passage in this case include: separation from being a girl, transition during the liminal period and reintegration as a woman.

Rites of passage are symbolic ways of changing the status of members of a society. Turner wrote, "I found I could not analyse ritual symbols without studying them in a time series in relation to other 'events' for symbols are essentially involved in social processes. I came to see performance of rituals as distinct phases in social processes whereby groups become adjusted to internal changes and adapted to their external environment. The symbol becomes associated with human interests, purposes, ends and means whether they are explicitly formulated or have to be inferred from the observed behaviour. The structure and properties of a symbol become those of a dynamic entity, at least within its appropriate context of action[1]."

Is the idea of liminal period relevant only for age-related transitions? Turner thinks not. He gives examples of pilgrimages in a complex society. Among Muslims, the status after Haj is higher compared to the status before Haj. Pilgrimage changes identity. During Haj, Muslims are in the liminal period.

During their liminal period, people, Turner said "are neither here nor there; they are betwixt and between the positions assigned and arrayed by law, custom, convention and ceremonial. As such, their ambiguous and indeterminate attributes are expressed by a rich variety of symbols in many societies that ritualize social and cultural transitions."

Liminal period positions people outside the normal structure. "If our basic model of society is that of structure of positions, we must regard the period of margin or 'liminality' as an inter-structural situation."

During the transitional stage between the structures, people can come under a collective identity. Turner called this ritual fusion of individuals into a collective identity 'communitas'. Muslims during Haj is an example. In India, Ayyappa devotees going to the Sabarimala temple constitute 'communitas'.

"Communitas is almost always thought of or portrayed by actors as a timeless condition, an eternal now, as 'a moment in and out of time' or as a state to which the structural view of time is not applicable. Such is frequently the character of at least parts of the seclusion periods found in many protracted initiation rites. Such is the character, too, I have found, of pilgrimages in several religions. In ritual seclusion, for example,

---

1 This section is based on *Visions of Culture* by Jerry D. Moore

one day replicates another for many weeks. The novices in tribal initiations waken and rest at fixed hours, often at sunrise and sunset, as in the monastic life in Christianity and Buddhism. They receive instruction in tribal lore, or in singing and dancing from the same elders or adepts at the same time. At other times they may hunt or perform routine tasks under the eyes of the elders. Every day is, in a sense, the same day, writ large or repeated."

So through symbols Turner is explaining the structure and the transitions across the structure. Turner knows that some people manipulate symbols in an unusual way to convey their position in the structure. "Those who would maximize communitas often begin by minimizing or even eliminating the outward signs of rank as, for example, Tolstoy and Gandhi tried to do in their own persons. In other words, they approximate in dress and behaviour the condition of the poor."

Gandhi tried to approximate the condition of the poor. So he dressed that way. Using this theory, we can understand why Ambedkar chose to dress differently and whom he was trying to approximate.

Are not people tired of the structure they are tied to? Do not they want to free themselves from the structure? Turner says that is what people do in a carnival! That is a liminal state in which everyday structure is dispensed with and normal identities and roles are inverted. This side of culture is expressed through ritual chaos during the liminal states. Turner calls this *antistructure*. This relief from the structure in the end only helps reinforce the structure. Remember the Monday morning after your college festival – back to the routine with renewed energy!

Social drama

Turner used the concept of 'social drama' to explain the conflict in the Ndembu society. He first got this idea when he was analysing a problem related to Sandombu, a sorcerer. Edith Turner, Turner's wife, wrote, "with controlled excitement he read the story of Sandombu and he analysed its stages – breach, crisis, redress, reintegration – the social drama as the window into Ndembu social organization."

Social drama is about how a norm is breached, and how it leads to a crisis and how it is resolved. "When the interests and attitudes of groups and individuals stood in obvious opposition, social dramas did seem to me to constitute isolable and minutely describable units of social process."

Social dramas are part of any society. In our society, take the example of a low-caste man eloping with a high-caste woman. It is a breach of caste rule, which lands the entire village in a crisis. How is that addressed? Caste council meets, delivers judgment. The punishment can be very severe. There are the procedures of redress "ranging from informal arbitration to elaborate rituals, that result either in healing the breach or public recognition of its irremediable character."

It is not that social dramas always lead to restoration of harmony. Schism is possible instead of reintegration. Note that the title of Turner's book about Ndembu is *Schism and Continuity in an African Society* (1957). Some social processes are based on cooperative efforts, rather than conflicts. Turner called them *social enterprises*.

Ritual symbolism

Turner's account of symbols in a Ndembu ritual as given

in his *The Forest of Symbols* (1967) throws light on his approach towards symbolism. Let us see how he explains *Nkanga* ritual and what he learns about the Ndembu society through this ritual.

The *Nkanga* ritual is related to a girl's puberty. The ceremony is held when the girl's breasts begin to ripen, not after her first menstruation which is the subject of a less elaborate ritual. When is something called a ritual? A ritual involves predetermined formal behaviour. A ritual is "prescribed formal behaviour for occasions not given over to technological routine having reference to beliefs in mystical beings or powers.[2]"

Any ritual consists of symbols. What is a symbol? "Symbol is the smallest unit of ritual which still retains the specific properties of ritual behaviour; it is the ultimate unit of specific structure in a ritual context." A symbol need not be only an object. Symbols can be "objects, activities, relationships, events, gestures and spatial units in a ritual situation." Symbols stand for certain aspects of culture. An anthropologist has to decipher what they stand for.

The Nkanga ritual takes place around *Mudyi tree*, conspicuous for its white latex which exudes in milky beads if the thin bark is scratched. Turner calls this *milk tree*. What is the significance of the milk tree? It is very significant. A specialist said, "The milk tree is the place of all mothers of the lineage. It represents the ancestress of both women and men. The milk tree is where our ancestress slept when she was initiated." So important is this tree that an educated Ndembu said, "Mudyi is our flag!"

---

2 This section is taken from Turner's article *Symbols in Ndembu Ritual* as given in *Anthropological Theory*.

Why is this tree so important? Turner thinks, "At one level of abstraction the milk tree stands for matriliny, the principle on which the continuity of Ndembu society depends." The tree symbolism is reinforcing the matriliny. This is a structural-functionalist explanation.

Turner thinks on closer examination that the ritual represents not only the social cohesion but social conflict also. During this ritual, women taunt men and deny them access to their dance circles. Turner takes this as ritual enactment of hostility between men and women. But the ritual enactment of conflict, as Gluckman said, does not disrupt the structure; rather it ends up supporting the structure.

Turner does not confine himself to structural functionalist explanations. He goes for psychological explanations too. In one part of the ritual, mother and daughter interchange portions of clothing. This is similar to the custom where mourners wear small portions of a dead relative's clothing. Turner writes, "This is one of the symbolic actions – one of very few – about which I found it impossible to elicit any interpretation in the puberty ritual. So "it is legitimate to infer, in my opinion, that powerful unconscious wishes, of a kind considered illicit by Ndembu, are expressed in it." He chooses Freud rather than L'evi-Strauss for psychological explanations. How Turner is able to make that conclusion is one point.

But a more important point is that Turner is willing to infer things that are not expressed by the natives. In other words, he is able to arrive at an etic view and not confine to the emic – though he did not use these terms.

Another notable point is that in analysing Nkanga, he is using the symbols used in some other ritual – in this case, sharing clothing. "Each kind of Ndembu ritual has several meanings and goals that are not made explicit by informants, but must be inferred by the investigator from the symbolic pattern and from behaviour. He is able to draw these inferences only if he has previously examined the symbolic configurations and meanings attributed to their component symbols by skilled informants, of many other kinds of ritual in the same total system."

Would not there be conflicting accounts of symbols? Turner thinks that is possible. "We may be able to speak legitimately of levels of interpretation, for a layman will give the investigator simple meanings, while specialists will give him esoteric explanations and more elaborate texts. Next, behaviour directed towards each symbol should be noted, for such behaviour is an important component of its total meaning."

Turner also thinks certain rituals in Nkanga reveal the tension between two aspects of the society: matriliny and virilocality. There is conflict over who takes first a large spoonful of cassava and beans. Women compete. Turner learns it is considered lucky if the spoon goes to the woman from the novice's own village. It meant the girl would stay in the village and not go to a different village because of virilocality. The quarrel among women – between the girl's matrilineal kin and those of the bridegroom – represents, to Turner, the conflict between matriliny and virilocality. In this context, the milk tree is described as representing the novice's matrilineage.

Conflicts such as these are part of the etic view. Informants are not aware of this. "My informants genuinely believed that the milk tree represented only the unifying aspects. I am convinced that it represents a focus of specified groups in opposition to other groups."

Interpreting symbols is the task of an anthropologist. If there is no interpretation at all, it is not a symbol! In this context, Turner quotes Carl Jung to whom "a sign is an analogous or abbreviated expression of a known thing. But a symbol is always the best possible expression of a relatively unknown fact, however, which is none the less recognised or postulated as existing."

An anthropologist should sift through different interpretations. Can he do that? Can he be objective? Turner thinks an anthropologist can be objective. That is what he is trained for. "We also become aware that a complex relationship exists between the overt and submerged and the manifest and latent patterns of meaning. As social anthropologists, we are potentially capable of analysing the social aspect of this relationship." In that sense, Turner is not a postmodernist.

Questions to think about

1. How did Turner explain rites of passage?
2. What are symbols? What are rituals?
3. What is liminal period?
4. What is meant by 'communitas'?
5. What is antistructure?
6. What is social drama?
7. What aspects of culture are revealed through the Nkanga ritual?
8. What is Turner's stand on emic and etic views of culture?
9. Is Turner a postmodernist?
10. What is meant by social cohesion?
11. How is structure related to liminality?
12. Think of certain symbols in Hindu society and explain what they signify.

24. Clifford Geertz

Clifford Geertz (1926-2006), an American anthropologist, is well-known for what is called 'interpretative approach' to the study of culture.

What is meant by interpreting culture? How is this approach supposed to be different from the previous ones? He will choose to study an important event and record many facts relating to it. He will also record various interpretations and give his own. Through the event, he wants to narrate what that society is. The features of this approach include:

1) Anthropologist is analysing the culture in terms of an event. He is studying an event, not just for the sake of the event, but to see how culture is expressed through it.

2) His report is only an interpretation and not the final truth. He makes no claim to finality.

3) There is no effort on his part to arrive at the laws of culture. Nor does he have any belief in arriving at the laws.

Who else supported the idea that culture was for

interpretation only? Max Weber was one. He believed that sociology was only an interpretative understanding of social action. Geertz was impressed by Weber's idea. "The concept of culture I espouse, and whose utility the essays below attempt to demonstrate, is essentially a semiotic one. Believing, with Max Weber, that man is an animal suspended in webs of significance he himself has spun, I take culture to be those webs, and the analysis of it to be therefore not an experimental science in search of law but an interpretative one in search of meaning[1]." The essays he was referring to were published under the title *The Interpretation of Culture* (1973).

Anthropology is not to be a science in search of law, but an interpretative discipline in search of meaning. He did not think any discovery of laws of culture is possible. "Human beings, gifted with language and living in history, are for better or worse, possessed of intentions, visions, hopes and moods, as well as of passions and judgments, and these have more than a little to do with what they do and why they do it. An attempt to understand their social and cultural life in terms of forces, machinations, and drives alone, objectivised variables set in systems of closed causality, seems unlikely to succeed."

Only interpretation is what is possible. According to Geertz, previously also anthropologists might be thinking that they were discovering laws. It was because they had not seen the bias in their observations and conclusions. "What we call our data are really our own constructions of other people's constructions of what they and their compatriots are up to. But this fact is obscured because most of what we need to comprehend a particular event, ritual, custom, idea, or whatever is insinuated as background information before the thing itself

---

1 All the quotations in this section are from *Visions of Culture.*

is directly examined. There is nothing particularly wrong with this, and it is in any case inevitable. But it does lead to a view of anthropological research as rather more of an observational and rather less of an interpretative activity than it really is."

How should an anthropologist go about interpreting a culture? It is through describing various aspects and viewpoints of an issue or an event. Geertz introduced this approach in an article *The Social History of an Indonesian Town* (1965). "The document (which might be called the 'example' or as this method is often referred to as clinical, the 'case') is seen as a particular embodiment, a specific manifestation of a more comprehensive pattern which has a very large, in some cases virtually infinite, number of such embodiments and manifestations, the one at hand simply being regarded as particularly telling in the fullness, clarity and the elegance with which it exhibits the general pattern. In it the paradigm is made flesh: the ineradicable specificity of actual events and the elusive generality of meaningful form render one another intelligible."

So an event can be taken and explained in detail. Geertz later called this *'thick description'*, a method borrowed from Gilbert Ryle, who said an event should be read from its context. Gilbert Ryle gave an example of how winking means different things in different contexts – what it means between a girl and a boy is different from what it means between a superior and a subordinate. One can't guess its meaning from the physical act. It has to be read in the context of what it meant to the participants. Only the physical act of twitching eyelids is the same but the meaning is context-dependent. The same is true of a cultural event. Its meaning is different to the people involved or to the various groups and the individuals.

This approach is a semiotic one. Semiotics is the analysis of signs and symbols. The word 'chair' is not a chair, it only stands for a chair. Chair is called differently in different languages. A translator does not question the use of the word 'chair', he simply records it and tries to see what it stands for. An anthropologist is like that. He tries to read a culture as a text. "Doing ethnography is like trying to read a manuscript – foreign, faded, full of ellipses, incoherencies, suspended emendations, and tendentious commentaries, but written not in conventionalized graphs of sound but in transient examples of shaped behaviour."

This approach is about anthropologists' interpretation of the interpretation of the informants! "To grasp concepts that, for another people, are experience-near and to do so well enough to place them in illuminating connection with experience-distant concepts theorists have fashioned to capture the general features of social life, is clearly a task at least as delicate, if a bit less magical, than putting oneself into someone's else's skin. The trick is not to get yourself into some inner correspondence of spirit with your informants. Preferring, like the rest of us, to call their souls their own, they are not going to be altogether keen about such an effort anyhow. The trick is to figure out what the devil they think they are up to."

What is the historical significance of the interpretative approach when compared to the previous ones? In the previous period, foreigners went to distant islands, stayed with the local people, observed them, came back as 'experts' to tell the world about the strange island people. But Anthropology was changing. The cultures one is studying are themselves complex, they have histories and more importantly, they are in a position to tell their stories to others. Anthropologists have understood that they can't behave like 'experts,' and their story is not final. So the interpretative approach is part of this humbling experience to anthropologists.

Balinese cockfight

Geertz went to Bali with his wife in 1958 to conduct fieldwork. The government ensured that they would stay in an extended family in a village. The way he described Balinese cockfight is an example of his 'thick description.' So let us see how he explained it.

First, as expected, he gives the simple facts of a cockfight. Any fight takes place between two cocks. Cockfights are arranged during afternoons. Fights go on for three to four hours till sunset. Four-to-five-inch-long steel spurs are affixed to their legs. The man who attaches spurs also provides them. Handlers may or may not be their owners. If a cock delivers a blow it is picked up. Fight to mutual death is avoided. The cock that dies first is declared the loser. There are elaborate rules regarding how to conduct a cockfight. Rules along with lore are passed on in palm-leaf manuscripts. The umpire's decision is final. Geertz never heard of any accusation of bias against the umpire.

What is the material outcome of the cockfight? First, the owner of the winning cock takes the carcass of the loser. Next, there is betting – sometimes very big amounts. Geertz calls fight with big amounts *deep play*. The bets are so high that in terms of Bentham's utilitarianism, the marginal disutility of losing money is higher than the marginal utility of gaining. Why then do people play? His answer is, 'esteem, honour, dignity'. In a *shallow game* money may be important, but in a deep one psychological variables are more important.

Who are these bettors? The main bet is between the owners. But the audience is also involved in betting. Geertz explores who is betting on which cock. Here he notices that men are not betting on their understanding of which cock is likely to win and what probability is there to make money. Alliances – kin and non-kin – determine on which cock one bets. You are not supposed to bet against the cock of your own kin group. If you think the other's cock is sure to win, the utmost you can do is avoid betting. To bet against the cock of your own group amounts to showing disloyalty to your own group. That village has four factions. Your membership of a faction can also determine which side you can bet. The village-level factions are not important if your village cock is fighting against the cock of another village. You can only bet on the one from your village. So betting alliances reflect alliances outside the cockfight.

People gather around cockfight and cheer. You can't find yourself cheering against your own group – be it kin group, faction or village.

Cockfights reveal not only horizontal grouping, but also hierarchical arrangements in the society. Around a cockfight area, there are a large number of sheer-chance-type gambling games (roulette, dice throw, coin-spin). Only women, children, adolescents and various sorts of people who do not fight cocks – the poor, the socially despised – play those games. Above them are the people who do not fight cocks but bet in small matches. Above them are those who fight cocks in small matches. Above them are… Geertz records "the migration of the Balinese status hierarchy into the body of the cockfight[2]."

---

2 From Geertz's article as it appeared in *Anthropological Theory* edited by McGee and Warms.

Geertz was not confined to social aspects. He analyses psychological variables too. "The cocks may be surrogates for their own personalities, animal mirrors of psychic form." Through their cocks, the men are participating in a fight. This seeming sport, Geertz says, is "a status bloodbath!"

But, is the status altered permanently through cockfights? 'No,' says Geertz. It is only temporarily enhanced or degraded. Nor do these fights redistribute income. It is only a case of money flowing across the bettors. All gains and losses are evened out in the long run. So this 'status bloodbath' does not alter the status forever! "The cockfight is really real only to the cocks – it does not kill anyone, castrate anyone, reduce anyone to animal status, alter the hierarchical relations among people."

What does this study show about Geertz's notion of culture? Geertz is not judging cockfight on the basis of his own cultural values. He is trying to read what it means to the natives. "As (to follow Weber than Bentham), the imposition of meaning on life is the major end and primary condition of human existence, that access of significance more than compensates for the economic costs involved." Geertz wants to know what a victory in cockfight means to the natives, and not to him. Culture is a shared code of meaning. Culture is a form of text. This text is what an anthropologist should decipher.

Can one take Geertz's description as the only text of Balinese culture? Or that many texts are possible? Geertz gives an interesting answer. He said a different text can come if somebody else makes a study of a different event. "The mass festivals at the village temples, which mobilize the whole local population in elaborate hostings of gods – songs, dances, compliments, gifts – assert the spiritual unity of village mates against their status inequality and project a mood of amity and trust. The cockfight is not the master key to Balinese life, any more than bull-fighting is to the Spanish people. What it says about that life is not unqualified nor even unchallenged by what other equally eloquent cultural statements about it."

"The culture of people is an ensemble of texts, themselves ensembles, which the anthropologist strains to read over the shoulders of those to whom they properly belong."

Can these texts contradict? Why not? "There is nothing more surprising than the fact that Racine and Moliere were contemporaries." (Both were French playwrights of the 17th century – Racine of tragedies, Moliere of comedies.] It means contradictory texts are possible. This shows that Geertz is moving towards postmodern vision that culture is an intersection of competing texts.

"Functionalism lives, and so does psychologism. But to regard such forms as 'saying something of something' and saying to somebody, is at least to open up the possibility of an analysis which attends to their substance rather than to reductive formulas professing to account for them," wrote Geertz. Reductive formulas are not for him.

Questions to think about

1. What are the salient features of Geertz's interpretative approach?
2. Is Geertz interested in discovering laws of culture? Explain.
3. What do you know about Max Weber's approach to culture?
4. What is the document method? When did Geertz write about this?
5. Does Geertz throw light on the case study method?

6. What is meant by 'thick description'?
7. What is meant by culture as text?
8. What is the semiotic approach?
9. What does Geertz say about Balinese culture through his description of cockfight?
10. What is positivism? How is it different from the interpretative approach ?
11. What are the postmodernist leanings in his study on cockfight?

25. David M. Schneider

David M. Schneider (1918-75) is known for his symbolic approach to anthropology. The symbolism that Schneider referred to is of a more fundamental kind, unusual and counter-intuitive.

How fundamental is this? Suppose a researcher asks a native man, 'Is she your wife?' If the native replies, 'yes.' The anthropologist is expected to know what 'wife' means. The researcher is not expected to ask, 'what does the word 'wife' mean?' But going by Schneider's approach, the researcher is supposed to ask that question and in fact investigate what 'wife' means in that culture.

What does 'wife' mean in a culture? What does 'marriage' mean? Who is a 'kin'? Whom do you consider a kin? What obligations does your 'kin' have towards you?

What is wife in one culture is not the same in another culture. 'Wife' is the symbol of a culturally specific relationship, which an anthropologist has to unravel. Culture is a system of symbols. The symbol has to be analytically derived from what people say and do.

Like other anthropologists, Schneider studied primitive people, the Yap of Pacific island in the 1940s, and wrote about them. But he became famous not for his Yap-based studies but what he wrote on his own culture: American Kinship: A Cultural Account (1968). In that book, he showed that, what we take for granted regarding kinship is not true and everything is symbolic in nature and the symbols vary across cultures. Earlier, kinship was assumed to be uniform, Schneider showed that it was not.

If kinship is not a system of objective meanings but a system of symbols that are culture-specific, then kinship becomes worthy of study even in an advanced society like the US. Whom Americans marry, whom they call by kin terms and what roles are assigned to them are all important aspects of American culture. One can't say that kinship study is important only in simple societies. This Schneider's work showed.

Schneider discusses one distinct rule in American culture. For remote consanguines as well as for relatives by marriage, the rule explicitly requires the individual to decide for himself whether a person who can be located in the genealogy is to be considered a relative at all and whether or not a kinship term can be used in referring to him or addressing him. The choice is based on the realities of the actual social relationship between the parties.

His study is based only on the interviews of 53 middle-class white families in Chicago with various religious and ethnic origins. So its applicability to the entire American culture has been questioned. But the idea that kinship too is a system of symbols is valid across cultures. Many feminist scholars extended his theory of kinship to the study of sex roles.

Questions to think about

1) What is Schneider's approach to the study of kinship?
2) Is every kin term only a symbol that varies from culture to culture?
3) Why is his approach more radical than that of other symbolic theorists?

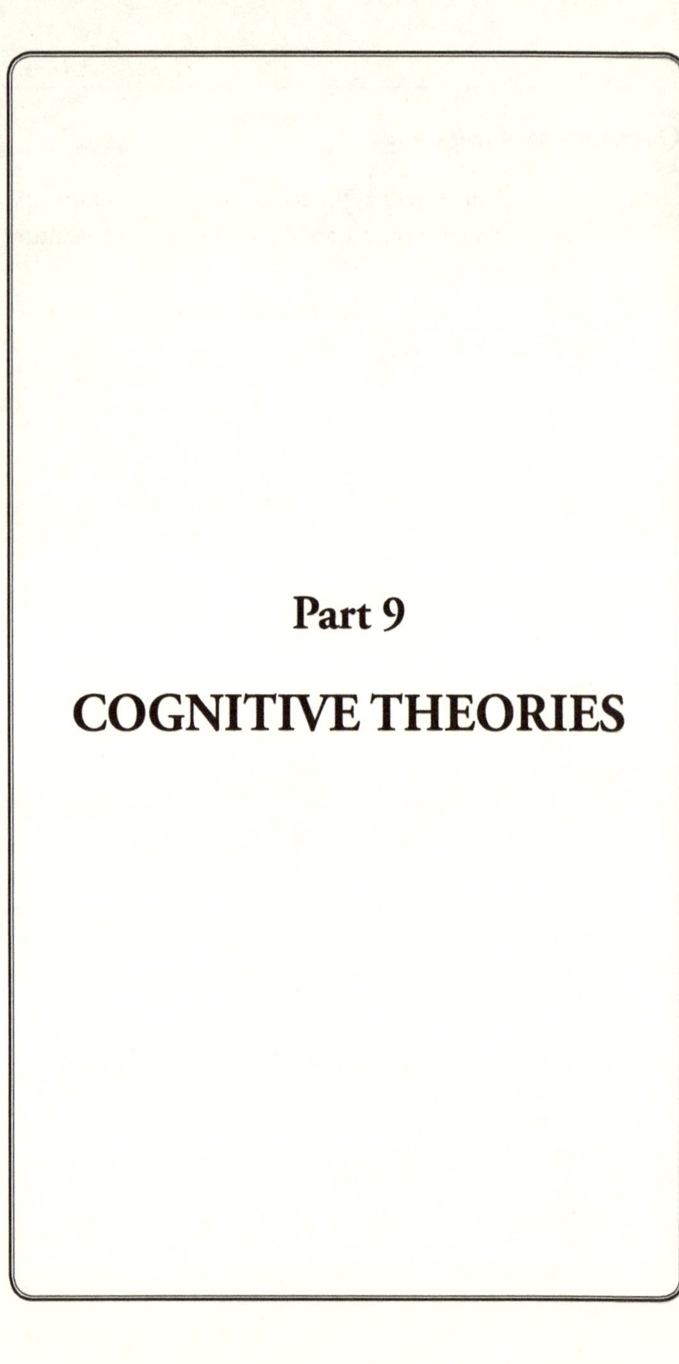

Part 9

COGNITIVE THEORIES

26. Emics and Etics

It is to differentiate the observer's point of view from the participants' point of view that many anthropologists have begun to use the terms "etic" and "emic". These words were introduced by the anthropological linguist Kenneth Pike in his book *Language in Relation to a Unified Theory of the Structure of Human Behavior*.

In gathering emic data, the observer attempts to acquire a knowledge of the categories and rules one must know in order to think and act as a native. For example, the researcher attempts to learn as to which rule lies behind the use of the same kin term for mother and mother's sister among the Bathonga or as to when it is appropriate to shame one's guests among the Kwakiutl. That is, the researcher in this methodology tries to explore the native's world view, his ways of looking at things.

Etic data is the (researcher's) observer's way of categorizing and describing culture. The observer may use concepts that are not in any way meaningful from the native's point of view. Etic data reveals how the researcher looks at the culture. Let us discuss an example that distinguishes emic data from etic data.

Marvin Harris found that in Kerala the mortality rate of male calves tended to be almost twice as high as the mortality rate of female calves. When Harris asked the farmers about the cause of death of the calves, they asserted that they would never kill or starve the calves to death since doing that would be a sin. Emics of the situation are that all calves had the right to live, regardless of sex. Etics of the situation are that males are culled and females reared. This is because in Kerala there is little demand for traction animals. This conclusion is also supported by the fact that in U.P. where oxen are very important, bovicide is practiced resulting in the sex ratio of 200 oxen for every 100 cows.

From the above example, don't wrongly conclude that emics deal with the mental field, and etics deal with the behavioral field. Mental-behavioral is one dimension and emic-etic is another dimension in the analysis. Going by Harris's distinction, Behavioral stream involves "all the body motions and environmental effects produced by such motions". Mental field involves "all the thoughts and feelings that people experience."

The example of bovicide can be put in the following way:

Emic/Behavioral	: No calves are starved to death.
Etic/Behavioral	: Male calves are starved to death.
Emic/Mental	: All calves have the right to life.
Etic/Mental	: Let the male calves starve to death when feed is scarce.

The theme of New Ethnography

The goal of New Ethnography is to arrive at a description and analysis of a culture as a member of that culture would see it. To put it simply, this is emic approach to the study of culture. New ethnography is also known as "Cognitive anthropology", or "Ethnoscience" or even as "Ethnosemantics."

Ethnoscientists study the language of natives, particularly the words the natives use to describe what they do. And then they try to formulate the rules that generate acceptable behavior in the culture. The rules in question are believed to be comparable to the grammatical rules that generate the correct use of language. Many ethnoscientists think that if we discover the rules that generate correct cultural behavior, we can explain much of what people do and why they do it.

Thus ethnoscientists or cognitivists try to discover rules and explain culture with the help of the rules. But they don't attempt to explain why or how those rules came about in the first instance. They take the entire emic sector as given and then attempt to probe it. And from the emic sector they try to explain or predict the etic sector. No consensus here. Some think predictions can be made, but some are less sure of the predictive adequacy of the etic sector from the emic sector. (Harris, 1979:266)

Ethnoscience is not identified with any single individual. Some of the anthropologists that belong to this school are: Kay, Ward Goodenough, Conklin, Frake, Wallace and Werner.

Harris's Criticism

Marvin Harris belongs to the school known as cultural materialism, which gives primacy to ecological and techno-economic factors and believes that both emic and etic data are important. It rejects any school that ignores etic data. Harris describes both structuralism and cognitivism as examples of cultural idealism for they gave priority not to material factors but to mental phenomena. The most important point Harris raises, (taking from his book *Cultural Materialism*) is that emic approach fails to predict socio-cultural phenomena.

Harris gives five reasons to explain predictive inadequacy of an exclusive emic approach.

1. Etic outputs require etic inputs: etic behavior can't be predicted simply from emic data.

Kay claims that etic behavior will correspond to rules if the rules are stated in terms of contingencies and alternatives. But in the case of predictions about residence patterns, he himself admits that "to predict distribution of actual residence patterns on an aggregate scale, we have to furnish as input to the postulated cognitive model the joint distribution of matri-sib membership, matri-sib localization, wealth in land and so on, for the entire population." But they are all etic inputs!

2. Emic rules are not free from ambiguity.

The whole effort of cognitivists is to find out emic rules, but rules are not the same to all the members of the society. There is considerable body of evidence to show that words are understood differently by members of the same speech community. Stephen Fjellman showed that kinship terminology is far from uniform in one single African culture. It means the rules that cognitivists depend upon so much are not uniform, i.e. not the same to all the members.

The ambiguity may have functional significance too. Stanley Freed has measured the degree of consensus concerning caste ranking in Uttar Pradesh. However, he did not consider the possible functional significance of the demonstrated lack of agreement in caste ranking. But it is clear to us that from Bernard Cohn's description of caste mobility through 'litigation' and 'violence' that such an ambiguity has a functional significance. (Harris, 1968:584) (Do you agree with this viewpoint? Analyze this from your understanding of Sanskritisation. Isn't ambiguity about the rank one of the stages that any caste passes through, before it moves up?)

166

Not enough research has been done to search out and quantify the actual extent of cognitive ambiguity and diversity.

3. For every emic rule, there is an alternative.

Cognitivists know that rules are broken, but they think they can identify the exceptions under which the rules are broken. That is, they think they can identify the rules for breaking the rules. In the island of Truk in Micronesia, Goodenough finds that fathers should 1.crouch or crawl if a married daughter is seated. 2. avoid initiating action in her presence 3. avoid speaking harshly to her. 4. honor any request and 5. never assault her "regardless of provocation". But Goodenough saw one father breaking all the five rules. The reason for this, Goodenough explained, was that "her petulant behavior had been getting on her kinsmen's nerves for some time." It was therefore "poetic justice". At this rate, there are many exceptions to any rule, one can't identify them. In other words, the rules for breaking rules are infinite.

4. There are no unchallenged authorities.

Goodenough admits that "no two persons in Truk have identical standards for what they regard as Trukese culture, and the amount of variance they accept in one another's behavior differs from one subject matter to another and from one kind of situation to another." But the solution to this problem of ambiguity and diversity depends upon the identification of individuals whom he calls "authorities", who are called upon to pronounce the truth when the standards are in dispute, and use them as the principal sources of information.

What Goodenough does not realize is that people obey rules endorsed by "authorities", not because they are obedient to rules, but because they are obedient to authorities. Actually there is so much of variation in the meanings people give to the rules that consensus is an illusion fostered by authorities. Also the interpretation of rules may take place in a way that is advantageous to the powerful in the society. Variation is the norm, and consensus may be an imposition.

5. Rules are not forever.

Cognitivists don't explain how long the rules remain the same, or why rules change at all. Nor do they have any idea of how the rules came into being in the first place. It is because they take the entire emic sector as given and do not link the emic sector to the etic sector to arrive at the causes of similarities and differences in socio-cultural life, which is precisely the strategy of cultural materialists.

My evaluation

I believe, any attempt to arrive at the science of culture should take both etic data and emic data into account; mere emic approach wouldn't do.

In any conversation, we wouldn't simply go by what others say, but we process it in a way intelligible to us. Ask your friend why he failed in the IAS exam. Suppose he says, "I am not lucky", do you simply accept that answer? Not likely. You will definitely process the answer in your own way and arrive at your answer that partly incorporates his answer. We can't blindly go by what others say without this constant processing at our level. Husband has an account of why his marriage broke, the wife has a different story to tell and we will not go by simply what they say, but we judge them by our experience of them and we may also take into others' evaluation of them and their relationship.

The point is that emic and etic data collection is no more

than a systematic extension of these basic cognitive processes applied to the study of culture. Emics is what the members of society think, etics is what the researcher thinks, going by his observations. He tries to bring order into an otherwise inconsistent and contradictory world – people say they wouldn't kill cows and yet highly unequal sex ratio is a fact. Etic data explains such inconsistencies, in a way that is meaningful to the scientific community.

Even if a researcher is wedded to the study of mental phenomena only, etic data is still useful because it provides insight even into mental phenomena. In the example of bovicide, the researcher can ask himself, why people go about ignoring the fact of bovicide. That may lead him to understand the power of traditions on the minds of the members.

I also believe that both structuralists and cognitivists have taken the analogy of language (to the culture) too seriously. Their point – just like we can discover acceptable ways of speech by the study of grammar, we can also find acceptable ways of behavior by studying rules of society – is based on many wrong assumptions.

The language aspect of a culture is far more arbitrary than other aspects of culture. The best way to study a language is to observe how the natives use it and try to learn it. No great purpose will be served by probing into how the word "chair" became the symbol of chair, or how is it that "childs" is wrong and "mothers" is right. Since language is arbitrary, it may be sufficient if we find out how natives speak, but the same is not true of behavior. Behavior has many reasons and it is not as arbitrary as language. If we were to ask why there is patriliny, or why people work so hard, there are reasons for it apart from what they say about why they are doing it. It is these reasons only pure emic orientation can never uncover.

Purely emic approach also assumes that people know why they are doing what they are doing. Many researches in psychology have revealed the role of unconscious motivation in any action. It will be difficult to uncover the why of anything purely with emic-oriented research.

To sum up, Emics is the proof of the respect the anthropologist gives to the natives and their world view. Etics is the proof of his own presence. A science of culture, if anything like that is possible, can never come into being by ignoring either type of data. To ignore is to enter a marathon race one-legged!

Questions to think about

1. What is the difference between emic and etic views? Who introduced these words?
2. How did Marvin Harris explain differences between emic and etic views using the example of bovicide in India?
3. What is the cognitivists' approach to emic data?
4. What reasons did Marvin Harris give against the exclusive emic approach?

27. Harold C. Conklin

Harold C. Conklin (1926-2016) was an American cognitive anthropologist. Cognitive anthropology studies cognitive processes that are specific to a culture. Cognitive processes refer to the processes within the mind as opposed to the processes in the external world.

Is there a relationship between what is in one's mind and what is outside? Of course, and a close one at that. But that relationship itself is culture-specific. How people perceive the world, how they categorize, how they think about is the subject of cognitive anthropology. One area of interest in this context is language. And the relationship between language and perception and thought is a worthy topic for investigation.

Conklin did linguistic fieldwork among the Hanunoo of the Philippines. He published his article *Hanunoo Colour Categories* in 1955. He classified their colour categories into Level I and Level II. Level 1 is basic and Level II is employed when greater specification is needed.

Level I includes 4 colours:

1.   *(ma) biru* – relative darkness of shades of colour – "includes the range usually covered in English by black, violet, indigo, blue, dark green, dark gray and deep shades of other colours"

2.   *(ma) lagti* – relative lightness of tint of colour, whiteness "white and very light tints of other colours and mixtures"

3.   *(ma) rara* – relative presence of red – maroon, red, orange, yellow and mixtures in which these qualities are seen to predominate

4.   *(ma) latuy* – relative presence of greenness – light green, and mixtures of green, yellow and light brown.

The first point is that Hanunoo categorization doesn't match with that of other cultures. Conklin noted that theirs did not match with the American one.

It definitely did not match with the scientific classification of colours. What is the scientific classification? It was based on spectral criterion. Red, green and blue are classified as primary colours. White is a combination of these three primary colours. Black is the absence of any colour.

In the Hanunoo system, Level I is based on two oppositions. One is between light and dark, obvious in the meaning of *biru* and *lagti*. This opposition may not be difficult to guess. The second opposition is not easy to guess. It relates to dryness or desiccation and wetness or freshness as reflected in *rara* and *latuy* respectively.

Is it not interesting that colour classification is influenced by dryness or wetness? Conklin wrote, "The basis of Level I classification appears to have certain correlates beyond what is usually considered the range of chromatic differentiation, and which are associated with nonlinguistic phenomena in the external environment[1]."

To eat a fresh fruit or vegetable is *pag-laty-un*. Dried-out plant material such as certain kinds of yellowed bamboo or hardened kernels or mature or parched corn are *marara*. To become desiccated, to lose all moisture is known as *mamara*.

This shows colour classification is influenced by what people consider important in their environment – whether something is dry or wet matters a lot to them.

In addition to those two oppositions, there is a third one – deep, unfading, indelible versus pale, faded, bleached. This opposition holds good for the manufactured as well as natural products.

Within each of these level 1 categories, increased aesthetic value is attached as the focal points are approached. With one exception, green. 'Green beads' are unattractive.

Level 2 terminology is employed only when greater specification is required. 'Somewhat mabiru', very 'mabiru' for example.

In Level 2, particular attention is paid to the texture of the surface which determines the degree and type of reflection (iridescent, sparkling, dull) and to the combination of other non-formal qualities. Frequently, these non-colorimetric aspects are considered to be of primary importance, and the spectrally-definable qualities are regarded as secondary attributes. In either

---

1 All quotations from Conklin's article given in *Anthropological Theory* by McGee and Warms.

case, polymorphemic descriptions are common.

Can there be gender differences in the colour categorization ability? There are. At Level 2, noticeable differences exist between men and women. Men excel in the ranges of reds and grays (animals, hair, feather) and women excel in 'blues' (shades of indigo-dyed fabrics). Must be due to differences in what they are more familiar with. However, no discernible difference holds for the 'greens' or 'whites'.

Questions to think about

1. Describe the colour categories of Hanunoo society.
2. How do ecological considerations influence colour categories?
3. How does culture influence colour categorization?
4. What is meant by cognitive anthropology taking Conklin's study as an example?

28. Stephen A. Tyler

"We have a pseudo-metalanguage. It is for this reason that nearly all ethnographies have similar chapter headings. The problem with this metalanguage is that it assumes universality without prior demonstration. Its universality inheres in the language of description and not necessarily in the object being described[1]," wrote Stephen A. Tyler in *Cognitive Anthropology* (1969), a collection of articles which he edited.

In ethnographies and in anthropology textbooks, we have similar headings. They are marriage, family, kinship, polity, religion etc. To Tyler, they constitute a pseudo-metalanguage. It is metalanguage because it is a language that is subsuming all the languages – languages of various cultures. Tyler is calling that language itself false, the very classification is false and misleading. Why so?

That classification is the anthropologists' way of analysing and classifying various cultures. The anthropologists have their own particular culture, a particular way of looking at things.

---

1 All quotations are from Tyler's article as given in *Anthropological Theory*.

They are observing and recording other cultures in the categories of their own culture. They are looking at other cultures through their own categories and modes of thought. What is universal is how they are describing the diverse cultures but what they are describing is not universal.

Through their own categories, through their own modes of thinking, anthropologists are only studying their own behaviour. "In a sense anthropologists were studying only one small culture – the culture of anthropology."

An anthropologist leaves an advanced society and goes to study the exotic. But he continues to think like one from the advanced society. He never learns about what the natives think of their society. He may spend time with them. He may do fieldwork. He may interview. But he sees them according to the mental categories of his own. This should stop, says Tyler.

Tyler argues that anthropologists should study how the natives understand their society. To understand the native point of view, an anthropologist should first understand how a native classifies the chaos around him. How does a native look at various objects, various processes and their relations? This approach is emic approach, as this is the native point of view. And this is cognitive approach because it tries to figure out what is going on inside the minds of the natives.

A cognitive anthropologist's study begins with discovering the native's way of finding order around him. "There are two ways of bringing order out of apparent chaos – impose a pre-existing order on it, or discover the order underlying it. Nearly all of earlier anthropology was characterized by the first method. By contrast, cognitive anthropology seeks to develop methods that can be used for discovering and describing these principles of organization."

How does one figure out what the native is thinking about the world around him? Tyler believes language is the key. Language is not simply a tool of communication. It is a way of perceiving, a way of thinking. Language is the key to the cognitive structures of the mind.

There is a lot in a name. it shows how we see things, how we relate things, in effect how we make sense of the chaos around us. "Naming is seen as one of the chief methods of imposing order on perception."

Semantic domains

Culture is seen as a mental construct consisting of some semantic domains. A semantic domain consists of a class of objects all of which share at least one feature in common which differentiates them from other semantic domains. 'Furniture' is a semantic domain. 'Livestock' is another semantic domain. Tables, chairs, sofas are some of the items under 'furniture'. Bulls, cows, horses, calves are among the 'livestock' items.

Items in a domain are arranged category-wise. This is called *taxonomy*. Taxonomy of 'livestock', for example, has cattle, horse, and sheep. Under cattle we have items such as cow, bull, calf. Under horse, mare and stallion. Under sheep, ram and lamb.

How is cow different from calf? The difference is age. How is a cow different from bull? The difference is sex. It means livestock is being classified not only under cattle, horse, sheep but also by sex and age. A stallion is an adult male horse. A mare is an adult female horse. Stallion and mare are both adult horses but their sex is different. One can draw a table of horse and cattle taking sex and age as two sides of the table. This is called *paradigm* of features for horse and cattle.

A semantic domain can also be represented in the structure of a *tree* – with roots and branches. This groups various items in terms of levels.

But how should a researcher identify the domains and the items? Tyler gives the method of *controlled eliciting* – which is using sentence frames derived from the language of the people. This involves making linguistically correct sentences with the items of the domain.   This method is different from using a questionnaire. In a questionnaire, the researcher uses predetermined categories. That mistake is avoided in controlled eliciting which not only gives answers but also helps him discover relevant questions.

Formal analysis is a method of stating the results of controlled eliciting. A formal analysis is complete when the relations among all the units comprising a semantic domain are described. Formal analysis emphasises internal consistency, completeness and form.

On culture

So what does a researcher get in the end? A cognitive description of a culture. How useful is this? Can one predict the behaviour of members of that society? Tyler does not think so. "There is no necessity to assume that the cognitive order is either systematically a derivative of or a predictor of substantive actions. Just as the grammar of a language provides no information on what all individual speakers will say on any given occasion, so too a cognitive description of a culture does not pretend to predict the actual behaviour of any individual."

178

If the study of culture can't 'pretend to predict' what then is the study for? Are we really aiming at anything? To Tyler, a study of a culture gives its cognitive picture and such studies give us the correct metalanguage. "What we need today is a more limited notion of culture which stresses theories of culture. Rather than attempt a general theory of culture, the best we can hope for at present is particular theories of cultures. These theories will constitute complete, accurate descriptions of particular cognitive systems. Only when such particular descriptions are expressed in a single metalanguage with known logical properties will we have arrived at a general theory of culture. Such a general theory will be equivalent to the language in which we describe cultures."

Cognitive studies should take us from pseudo-metalanguage to correct meta-language! The anthropology textbooks will not have the present chapter headings. They will be completely new. That should make a good beginning to get more relevant data which is comparable across cultures.

"Explicit here is a view of culture derived from a kind of ethnography in which the methods of description are public and replicable, and the results predictive of expectations of appropriate behaviour. Implicit is the cognitive reorganization of our categories of description and analysis. Cognitive anthropology entails an ethnographic technique which describes cultures from the inside out rather than from the outside in. Categories of description are initially derived from relevant features in a culture rather than from the lexicon of anthropology."

Tyler wants new categories, new language. The present one is not the correct one. The present comparative method is not correct because it is not comparing the similar. "Comparisons between systems can only be useful if the facts compared are truly comparable and we can not know what facts are comparable until the facts themselves are adequately described. When this is achieved, the units of comparison will be formal features rather than substantive variables."

And the present definition of culture serves no useful purpose. "Culture, conceived as the totality of human behaviour, ideas, history, institutions and artefacts has never been particularly useful as a meaningful method of explaining ethnographic facts. As a device which purports to explain all of man's learned behaviour, motivations, prehistoric record, ecological adaptations, biological limitations, and evolution it attempts too much. What we need is a more limited notion of culture which stresses theories of culture. These theories will constitute complete, accurate descriptions of particular cognitive systems."

So Tyler is aiming at some mega idea, whose source is mental. "It seems likely that the logical operations underlying principles of ordering are finite and universal, but capable of generating an infinite number of possible specific orderings. In this limited sense, cognitive anthropology constitutes a return to Bastian's search for the psychic unity of mankind."

But neither Tyler nor other cognitive anthropologists went anywhere near discovering such universal culture-producing cognitive structures. Moreover, if a study of one cognitive system can't 'pretend to predict' behaviour, how can a generation of a metalanguage and data-gathering around that metalanguage 'pretend to predict' behaviour? Does it not seem fruitless?

Whatever be the reasons, Tyler found himself moving towards postmodernism abandoning the cognitive anthropological orientation.

Questions to think about

1. What, according to Tyler, is the aim of a researcher studying a culture?
2. What do you know about semantic domain?
3. Explain what is meant by formal analysis.
4. What are the problems in the questionnaire method?
5. What are the problems in the comparative method?
6. Does Stephen Tyler agree with E.B. Tylor's definition of culture?
7. What is the final goal of cognitive anthropology? Has it reached that goal? Evaluate.
8. What is the purpose of Tyler's cognitive approach?
9. Why did he call the present anthropology pseudo-metalanguage?
10. Can a study of a cognitive structure predict culture?
11. Is cognitive approach emic approach?
12. Why do cognitive theorists insist on the emic approach?

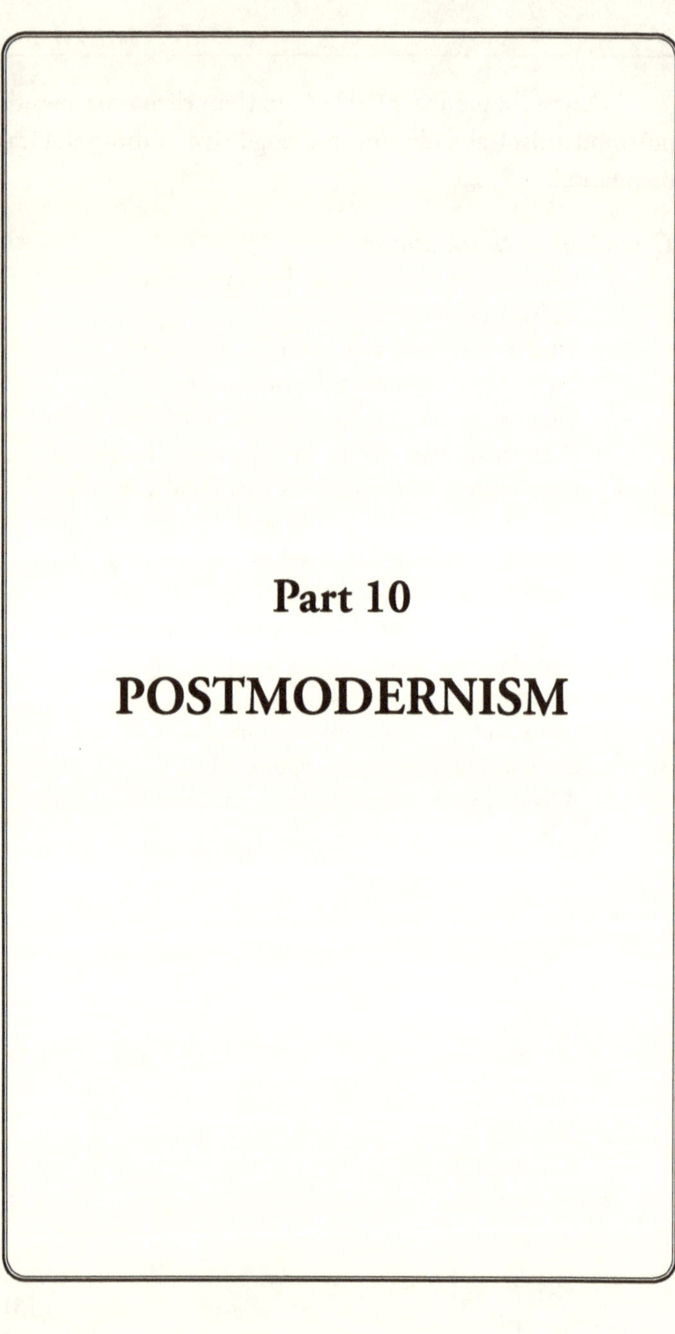

Part 10

POSTMODERNISM

29. Carlos Castaneda

Assumptions

"Truth is never a feature of the sensations of a discrete individual; it is always to be recognized in the knowledge of members of communities… Truths are always recognized with (as) the systems of intelligibility of a community. Truths are always for and within a community." – Silverman

Reflect on Silverman's quotation given above. That approach is called phenomenological approach. What do you feel about it? Are truths "always for and within a community?" Or do they have independent status, regardless of what we think?

The phenomenological approach in social sciences was founded by Edmund Husserl, a neo-Kantian. He drew a sharp line between the physical sciences and social sciences.

He said that the methodology used to study natural sciences is not applicable to study socio-cultural phenomena. Because social acts involve a property not present in other sectors of the universe – namely, the property of meaning. According to Husserl, meaning can be understood only subjectively. Hence to understand social acts, one must understand what they mean as subjectively, "lived experience". By assuming that the subjective experiences of others are similar to one's own, observers can draw analogies between their own intentions and goals and those of other actors and in this way begin to explain social life.

Phenomenologists deny the possibility that etic behavior stream actions are worth studying independently of the actor's meaning and purpose. "Social actions are meaningful actions and that is…they must be studied and explained in terms of their situations and their meanings to the actors themselves." (Jack Douglas)

Phenomenologists reject the possibility of separating the observers from the observed. Observation itself is to be approached as a lived experience in which the subjective meanings of both the observer and the participant are constantly "reflected" on. Moreover, the participant observer can never find the truth of the lived experience, apart from the consensus about such things found in the community in which the observer participates. Truths are always relative and social.

This philosophy of Husserl was transmitted through the writings of Alfred Schutz and formed the foundation of ethnomethodology and symbolic interactionism.

The problem of multiple truths

Before discussing ethnomethodology in detail, I would like to discuss a Japanese movie which raises the same issue – the problem of multiple truths. In the movie Rashomon, the viewer witnesses four different versions of the "same" scene. The principal actors are a man, his wife, a stranger and an onlooker hidden in the bushes. Each of these actors narrates a different version of the lived experience and each version appears on

184

the screen as the lived reality. Manly heroism in one version is depicted as abject cowardice in another; chastity in one is depicted as carnal venality in another. Each narrative unfolds as a graphic, vivid reality and the audience is left to decide on its own, which version, if any, actually represents the event – or indeed, if there ever was an "event" to begin with.

The cultural materialist considers that either only one version is etically correct or all are etically false. That is, he believes that there can't be many truths, there is only one truth.

But to a phenomenologist, all versions are equally true; for in his strategy etics are not distinguished from emics. If the participants are not lying (note the assumption), then what they saw within their systems of intelligibility must be accepted as true.

What is your opinion of the movie? Do you agree with the phenomenologists? Or with the cultural materialists? Or is there a different way of approaching the problem?

Carlos Castaneda

At the University of California, Castaneda studied under the ethnomethodologist Harold Garfinkel, in turn a student of Alfrez Schutz. Inspired by his phenomenological mentors, Castaneda resolved to do fieldwork that would involve him in the symbols and conventional meanings of a lived experience entirely different from that of Western social reality.

The Yaqui Indians provided Castaneda with a suitably exotic context for studying the 'separate reality' of another culture, especially as he had singled out to penetrate and participate in the most exotic aspect of this culture – the activities and thoughts of the community of Yaqui sorcerers and shamans.

Castaneda reports that Yaqui shamans believe they can fly through the air, change into animals, kill an adversary by sorcery and see through opaque objects. None of this may be news. Many earlier anthropologists have provided such accounts. But the difference is that Castaneda tells his story from the "inside", deliberately letting the emics and his own subjective feelings dominate the narrative. The aim of the narrative is to get the reader to participate in the shaman's system of intelligibility and thereby to demonstrate that reality is the creature of social consensus. If we can be persuaded to participate in the shamanic consensus, we will believe that shamans can fly.

Castaneda presented the shamanic experiences as an insider, as the one who was trained by Don Juan, a Yaqui shaman. But Castaneda did not give any etic details. Many doubts were raised whether Don Juan really existed or was only a character created by Castaneda. Castaneda never tried to answer these questions. Many of his followers say it does not matter whether Don Juan really existed or not. As David Silverman puts it, "It does not matter to me in the least whether any or all of the events reported by Castaneda ever 'took place'". To Silverman, any phenomenological account is interesting in its own right.

Harris's Criticism

"Cultural materialism is committed to getting closer and closer to this etic reality: phenomenology is committed to getting further and further away from it." – Harris.

Marvin Harris remains scornful about the whole issue of multiple truths. About the Japanese movie Rashomon, he says either all are false or only one is true. He says, we may not always find truth but truth is only one. In his words, "It does not follow from our inability to obtain absolutely certain knowledge that all knowledge is equally uncertain."

Sukenick said, "all versions of 'reality' are of the nature of fiction. There's your story; my story, there's the journalist's story and the historian's story… Our common world is only a description… reality is imagined." Harris thinks such an attitude is "an invitation to intellectual suicide". He further writes, "Does Sukenick seriously believe that all versions of reality are fictions? If so, then he believes his version of reality is a fiction. Since he believes that everything he says is fiction including what he says about reality, only a fool would believe such a man about anything."

Harris thinks belief in multiple truths leads not only to intellectual suicide, but also to moral depravity.

He writes, "The absolute precondition for any kind of moral judgement is our ability to identify who did what to whom, when, where, and how. The doctrine that fact is fiction and that all fiction is fact is a morally depraved doctrine. It is the doctrine that conflates the attacked with the attacker, the tortured with the torturer and the killed with the killer."

Emics and Etics

"All knowledge is ultimately emic." – Fisher & Werner.

To some, the issue of multiple truths may look like a philosophical one without much relevance to anthropological thought. But I don't think so and that is why we are discussing this issue. If we believe that there are many versions of 'reality', then it can be argued that what anthropologists discover is only one of the several possible versions. And what they call etics is really their own emics. Is not it? After all, who are the observers? Why should their own categories and beliefs be more credible than those of actors?

Harris is definitely against the view expressed by Fisher and Werner that all knowledge is ultimately emic. Harris thinks that "to urge that the etics of the scientific observers is merely one among an infinity of other emics – the emics of Americans and Chinese, of women and men, of Jews and Hindus…is to urge the surrender of our intellects to the supreme mystification of total relativism." To Harris, "to deny the validity of etic descriptions is in effect to deny the possibility of a social science capable of explaining socio-cultural similarities and differences."

My evaluation

At the outset let me make it clear, I agree with Harris that both emics and etics are important in the study of any culture. I have dealt with this elaborately in the topic on New Ethnography. My disagreement is – I believe etics is only one of the emics, one version of reality.

Castaneda probed a different system, which is consistent in its own way and according to which people can even fly – physically. The belief that flying is possible does not fit in our world view; we are very sure from our knowledge of the principles of physics that flying is not possible. But aren't we also trying to fly, albeit in other different ways?

When an anthropologist believes – like Harris does – that science of culture is possible, what is the basis of his belief? How is it different from Yaqui shaman's belief that he can fly? Marxists believed in the historical inevitability of Communism and explained how laws of history would ultimately take all societies towards it. They have maintained this belief against so much of evidence to the contrary. Is not their belief the same as Yaqui shaman's belief that he can fly?

The point is, man flies, societies fly; the only difference is the world into which they attempt to fly. Therefore, the difference between Marvin Harris and Yaqui shaman is not that one is scientific and the other is not, but that the communities to which their respective fantasies are addressed are not the same – they have different systems of intelligibility.

The significance of Castaneda's work is that it clearly points out the universality of human experience.

Changing emics of the scientists

Not only that laws of science change, but even the methodologies and criteria of validity change. For example, for a long time scientists believed that something existed or not existed, now, as they are influenced by the developments in quantum mechanics, they accept different degrees of existence. For a long time, scientists believed that a theory should be able to predict accurately in all instances. They now accept uncertainty as part of nature and only expect prediction in more number of cases to accept that a theory is good. In the words of Karl Person, one of the founders of mathematical statistics, "provable is the probable… Proof is the demonstration of overwhelming probability."

Not only do theories change, but the criterion of acceptability also changes. If scientists are involved in finding "etics", the truth, why should it change? Etics is only emics of the scientific community at a particular time. Scientists' methods of knowing are only one of the ways of knowing. Hence there is nothing offensive if someone were to say that "all knowledge is ultimately emic."

We have long ago accepted the concept of cultural relativism. We should accept that relativism applies not only to marriage systems and political and religious systems but also to systems of acquiring knowledge. In that sense, scientists' way of acquiring knowledge is not free from relativism.

Acceptance of epistemological relativism need not, and should not, prevent us from carrying our own "etic" study of cultures, just as the concept of cultural relativism didn't stop us from improving the lives in many simple societies. On the other hand, the acceptance of relativism should make us more aware of the limitations of our work.

An anthropologist is only a cultural translator. Etics is his translation of the culture he studies, to the scientific community in the way that is intelligible to it. Every anthropologist should understand this. Science of culture will not come into being ignorant of the assumptions on which it is built.

An update

Carlos Castaneda (1925-98), on whom Marvin Harris spent considerable time debunking in his *Cultural Materialism*, is currently not regarded as an anthropologist. Professor William W. Kelly, chairman of Yale's anthropology department, said, "I doubt you will find an anthropologist of my generation who regards Castaneda as anything but a clever con man. It was a hoax and surely Don Juan never existed as anything like the figure of his books. Perhaps to many it is an amusing footnote to the gullibility of naïve scholars, although to me it remains a disturbing and unforgivable breach of ethics[1]."

Now we know that Castaneda's *The Teachings of Don Juan* (1968) is a fiction. He submitted that fiction to the anthropology

---

1 From an article 'The dark legacy of Carlos Castaneda' by Robert Marshall published in Salon.com in 2007. BBC documentary on Castaneda is very well done.

department at UCLA. After that book became popular, he wrote *A Separate Reality, Journey to Ixtan* and *Tales of Power.* They too became popular. The books describe that he became an apprentice under a Yaqui sorcerer and learnt an entirely new way of perceiving and relating to the world. He perceived new reality first with peyote, a hallucinogenic plant, and later without drugs. He wrote that he experienced a new level of reality – in which he could talk to coyetes, can turn into a crow and fly! His books sold 10 million copies during his lifetime. A sizable number of people believed him that he could start a cult promising new reality to his followers.

A new level of perceiving the world is perfectly possible. A sorcerer might be having such an understanding. Simple societies may have something to teach about it. But an anthropologist, as an anthropologist, should maintain a distinction between fiction and nonfiction, make public his field notes (barring privacy issues) and discuss his methods of conclusion. Castaneda did not do these things. Had he presented his books as fiction, he would not have been successful in starting a cult which adversely affected many lives. Soon after his death, four of his close women followers are believed to have committed suicide -- at least one of them as per the plan he himself had given.

Castaneda may be a trickster. He may not be an anthropologist in the true sense of the word. But he is one man who used the knowledge system of the natives to question the knowledge systems of the modern world and enlighten it. Fiction or nonfiction, millions continue to read him.

Questions to think about

1. What is the phenomenological approach? To which philosopher can you trace its roots?
2. How do phenomenologists view the etic approach?
3. What is the phenomenological approach to truth?
4. What are the influences on Castaneda?
5. Who is Don Juan?
6. What is Harris's criticism of Castaneda?
7. Can Castaneda be regarded as an anthropologist? Explain.

30. Feyerabend

"The need to wait and ignore large masses of critical observations is hardly ever discussed in our methodologies," wrote Paul Feyerabend, an Austrian philosopher of science. Interesting, isn't it?

The major works of Feyerabend (1924-94) include *Against Method* (1975), *Science in Free Society* (1978) and *Farewell to Reason* (1987). He is an influential figure in the sociology of scientific knowledge. The Asteroid (22356) is named in his honour.

We have heard of the need to not ignore a critical observation to see if a theory may be disproved by it. And we have heard that if any fact disproves a theory, then that theory stands invalid. A black swan disproves the theory 'all swans are white'. We are told that the theory 'all swans are white' is true until a black swan is found. Once a black swan is found, we should discard the old theory. That is why we are told to pay attention to every possible fact, every critical observation that might disprove. But Feyerabend is saying just the opposite! Talking about the need to wait and ignore large masses of critical observations!

Karl Popper said something is science only when it is falsifiable. It means that only when a theory can be disproved by a fact when it is wrong is a science. Astronomy is a science, astrology is not. Nor is vastu a science, as per Karl Popper. Why so? Because astrology or vastu is not falsifiable. If a prediction does not come true, the astrologer will not say astrology is wrong but blames the result on other factors. If one constructs a house according to perfect vastu, the vastu pandit will not guarantee that nothing bad will ever happen to the inmates. Vastu, he will say, only reduces malefic influence. It means vastu is not falsifiable, astrology is not falsifiable. So they are not sciences. Thus went Karl Popper's argument.

Feyerabend would not agree. A theory can ignore a large mass of facts; a theory need not explain a large mass of facts and yet the theory might be right. So falsifiability is not the criterion.

Why should Feyerabend take such an unusual position? He came to such a conclusion after reading the history of Science. Take the case of Galileo. We have read that Galileo stood for observation and reason and the Church stood for belief and faith in The Bible. Feyerabend looked at the event differently. He says what Galileo had said was not as per the science known at that time. Science at that time, not just the Bible, contradicted Galileo.

If, as claimed by Galileo, the earth is revolving how come that a stone thrown from the top of the tower falls exactly below on the earth? This was called *tower argument* put forward to disprove that the earth was moving. Like the tower argument, there were many pieces of scientific observations that did not fit in with Galileo's theory.

Galileo's theory was unscientific given what science then

was. Feyerabend concludes, "The church at the time of Galileo was much more faithful to reason than Galileo himself, and also took into consideration the ethical and social consequences of Galileo's doctrine. Its verdict against Galileo was rational and just.[1]" So what is considered unscientific at one time may not be wrong, and may be accepted as scientific later.

If we kill a new theory because it is not consistent with the old theories, it will be difficult for new theories to emerge. New theories need not be consistent with the old ones. "The consistency condition is unreasonable because it preserves the older theory, and not the better theory." Nor should a theory be consistent with all the known facts. The new theory may in future explain them, do not reject it now on the ground that it can't explain all. "The methodological unit to which we must refer is a whole set of partly overlapping, factually adequate, but mutually inconsistent theories." Feyerabend wants mutually inconsistent theories!

Rejection of falsification, mutual inconsistency, unexplainable facts… This is his vision of science. Feyerabend is saying it is not just his vision of what it should be. He is saying it was what the science had been. Science did not develop logically and linearly. It developed through revolutions.

He draws these lessons from Thomas Kuhn's *The Structure of Scientific Revolutions* (1962). Science goes through certain paradigms. In each paradigm, certain questions are asked, certain methods are permitted, certain conclusions are made. Then something completely new happens, the old paradigm is broken and a new one begins. Science developed that way.

---

1 The quotations are from Feyerabend's *Against Method* as summarized by Tomas Petricek.

In each paradigm only certain things were regarded as scientific and other things unscientific, though they were not wrong. Feyerabend argues that scientists often miss this point. Living in a paradigm, they do not see the limitations of that paradigm. Among the scientists "Scepticism [about established science] is at a minimum. It is directed against the view of opposition and against minor ramifications of one's own basic ideas, never against the basic ideas themselves. Attacking the basic ideas evokes taboo reactions which are no weaker than are taboo reactions in so-called primitive societies."

He was particularly critical of the generation of scientists that emerged after World War II. He regretted that these scientists missed the philosophy of science. "The withdrawal of philosophy into a "professional" shell of its own has had disastrous consequences. The younger generation of physicists, the Feynmans, the Schwingers etc. may be very bright; they may be more intelligent than their predecessors, Bohr, Einstein, Schrodinger and so on. But they are uncivilized savages, they lack in philosophical depth – that is the fault of the very same idea of professionalism which you are now defending." To Feyerabend, Feynman was an uncivilised savage!

Feyerabend wants creative search for theory, unrestricted by what is regarded as a scientific method. "To those who look at the rich material provided by history, it will become clear that there is only one principle that can be defended under all circumstances: it is this principle: anything goes." He clarifies, "Anything goes is not a 'principle' I hold… but the terrified exclamation of a rationalist who takes a closer look at history."

"The alternatives may be taken from the past as well. As a matter of fact, they may be taken from wherever one is able to find them – from ancient myths and modern prejudices, from the lucubrations of experts and from the fantasies of cranks."

"There is no rule of thumb for distinguishing good and bad science. Epistemological anarchism is more likely to encourage progress than its law-and-order alternatives."

On language

Feyerabend makes interesting observations on language too. He says scientists should choose the language that frees the people from thinking in older ways. "The language in which we express our observations may have to be revised so that the new cosmology is not endangered by an unnoticed collaboration of older ideas."

Evaluation

Epistemological anarchism should not mean any method can be correct, nor should it mean all methods are equally correct. But Feyerabend said things which imply that science is only as good as any other belief system.

He believed that like other religious ideologies, science also was an ideology and it should not be imposed on a plural society. In Science in a Free Society, he envisioned a "free society" in which "all traditions have equal rights and equal access to the centres of power." By that token, state should treat homeopathy on a par with modern medicine!

Surely that would not be a correct stand to take. Scientific method can be judged by the results it produces – be it technology, or superior explanation. Instead of science imitating a religious ideology in a plural society, religious ideology should emulate science – that is accepting the scrutiny of the evidence rather than public opinion.

Fight against the tyranny of a method does not imply that all other methods are equally good and so let people choose the method of their choice. If science has progressed, it is because it was less tied to public opinion.

Questions to think about

1. What is the relevance of Feyerabend to a theory of culture?
2. What is the problem in taking falsifiability as the criterion of science?
3. What, according to Feyerabend, are the lessons that one can learn from Thomas Kuhn's *The Structure of Scientific Revolutions?*
4. What is tower argument?
5. Should a new theory be consistent with the old one?
6. Should a theory explain all the known facts?
7. What is meant by epistemological anarchism?
8. Should a scientific method be subjected to democratic control?
9. Are scientific methods equally valid?

31. Bruce Lee: No Way As Way

Bruce Lee (1940-73) was not simply a great martial arts expert. He was a philosopher of martial arts. What he said about styles in martial arts appears very relevant to schools in anthropology. Lee's observations on how a fighter should approach his opponent tell us how a researcher should study a culture. Lee's observations on what a student should be taught seem relevant to any trainee anthropologist.

How did Lee arrive at his philosophy that went beyond the realm of martial arts? He studied a lot, thought a lot. And of many people he read, J. Krishnamurti stands topmost among the people who shaped Lee's thought.

Bruce Lee was first trained in Kung Fu. After that he explored other styles. Unsatisfied with the existing styles, he wanted to evolve a new style. And then he realized that any style, no matter how perfect, has its limitations. He then evolved a philosophy which can be summed up as: "Using no way as way; using no limitation as limitation."

Where does one come across Krishnamurti's influence here? I think if not for Krishnamurti, Lee would most probably have evolved a distinct style and advocated it. He might have championed one style. In fact, he had been developing one style before becoming critical of the very concept of a style – Jeet Kune Do, the Way of Intercepting Fist, was what he had been advocating at one time.

Lee's rejection of all styles is similar to Krishnamurti's rejection of all religions. To Krishnamurti, any religion, any approach, any path, any method only conditions the mind. So he came to say, "Truth is a pathless land." This influenced Lee to think similarly about the styles of martial arts.

Why did Krishnamurti seem very relevant to Lee? Lee had found that people were more interested in perfecting a style, which had been taught in the same manner for thousands of years, without paying attention to the complexity and reality of the situation. The learners were more faithful to the tradition than to the situation they were facing.

Lee saw so much gap between what was being taught and the complexity of the real fighting. Even in a tournament, points were awarded to those who gave a particular punch and judges gave points on their understanding of how much hurt it would have caused if the punch had actually been delivered. Lee found that all this was hopelessly out of touch with reality. He found that they were all perfecting a system of strokes without ever questioning its relevance. Lee also found that many items were redundant, ineffective and ornamental. So he chose to evolve something simple, honest and direct.

What Lee said on styles

"An intelligent mind is one which is constantly learning, never concluding – styles and patterns have come to conclusion, therefore they have ceased to be intelligent."

200

"If you want to understand the truth in martial arts, to see any opponent clearly, you must throw away the notion of styles or schools, prejudices, likes and dislikes, and so forth. Then, your mind will cease all conflict and come to rest. In this silence, you will see totally and freshly."

"A conditioned mind is never a free mind. Conditioning limits a person within the framework of a particular system."

"Set patterns, incapable of adaptability, only offer a better cage. Truth is outside all patterns."

"To express yourself in freedom, you must die to everything of yesterday. From the 'old' you derive security; for the 'new', you gain the flow."

"One can function freely and totally if he is 'beyond system'. The man who is really serious, with the urge to find out what truth is, has no style at all. He lives only in what is."

"The wheel revolves when it is not too tightly attached to the axle. When the mind is tied up, it feels inhibited in every move it makes and nothing is accomplished with spontaneity. Its work will be of poor quality or it may never be finished at all."

"The mind must be wide open to function freely in thought. A limited mind can't think freely."

"When you are uninfluenced, when you die to the conditioning of classical responses, you will know awareness and see things totally fresh, totally new."

"To see a thing uncoloured by one's own personal preferences and desires is to see it in its own pristine simplicity."

Style and ego

Why does a man pursue a style rather than be devoid of all styles? A style involves repetition, a particular comprehension of reality and a predetermined response to it. This is a source of security. It makes one feel 'Yes, I know how it is going to be and I will handle it.' Krishnamurti thinks this idea of certainty and habit of responding from the past is rooted in one's ego. Lee understood this too and said things that are critical of ego.

"Because one's self-consciousness or ego-consciousness is too conspicuously present over the entire range of his attention, it interferes with his free display of whatever proficiency he has so far acquired or is going to acquire. One should remove this obtruding self or ego-consciousness and apply himself to the work as if nothing were taking place at the moment."

"Art reaches its greatest peak when devoid of self-consciousness. Freedom discovers man the moment he loses concern over what impression he is making or is about to make."

"The consciousness of self is the greatest hindrance to the proper execution of all physical action."

"It is the ego that stands rigidly against influences from outside, and it is this 'ego rigidity' that makes it impossible for us to accept everything that confronts us."

"When the mind is fluid, it moves in response to ten thousand situations but remains ever the same."

"Empty your mind. Be formless, shapeless. Like water. If you put water in a teapot, it becomes a teapot. If you put it in a cup, it becomes a cup. Be water."

"Flow in the total openness of the living moment. Moving, be like water. Still, be like a mirror. Respond like an echo."

"The oak tree is mighty. Yet it will be destroyed by a mighty wind because it resists the elements; the bamboo bends with the wind, and by bending it survives."

"You want to learn the way to win, but never to accept the way to lose. To learn to die is to be liberated from it. You must free your ambitious mind and learn the art of dying."

What should a teacher be?

Krishnamurti's opposition to the concept of a Guru also influenced Lee. Awareness can't be taught. One can teach *a* way but not *no* way. "I can't teach you, only help you explore yourself," is the position Lee took on training students.

Contradictions within?

How can one understand the dynamite of martial arts speaking on limitations created by ego? A man who has renounced the material world can speak about the limitations of ego. How can a fighter, whose performance is apparently based on unleashing of aggression, be critical of ego? Are not there contradictions in Lee? Is not aggression, sourced in ego, the very basis of Lee's tons of practice?

We need not expect explicit resolution of the contradictions from a 30-plus-year-old fighter, but we may be benefited from knowing what he thought of these contradictions.

- "The yielding will has a reposeful ease, soft as downy feathers; a quietude, a shrinking from action. An appearance of inability to do. (The heart is humble, but the work is forceful.) placidly free from anxiety, one acts in harmony with nature; one moves and revolves in the line of creation."

- "A self-willed man has no other aim than his own growth. He values only one thing, the mysterious power in himself which bids him live and helps him grow. His only living destiny is the silent, ungainsayable law in his own heart, which comfortable habits make it so hard to obey but which the self-willed man is destiny and godhead."

- "Instead of dedicating your life to actualize a concept of what you should be like, actualize yourself. The process of maturing does not mean to become a captive of conceptualization. It is to come to the realization of what lies in our innermost selves."

It appears, to Lee, effort is not in overcoming self, but realizing it. Water is not working *hard* in flowing. Bamboo is not working *hard* in bending.

Extended, Nietzsche's hero would not be working hard fighting battles. Nor was Howard Roark, Ayn Rand's hero, working hard as an architect. Self-expression does not require effort. Only the tasks that are not self-expressions require effort, because they have to overcome resistance. So it seems. Surely Krishnamurti was not exerting himself lecturing.

Bruce Lee's life raises tremendously significant questions on the issues of aggression, effort and limitations of ego. Those who renounced the world advocated certain philosophies which seemed anti-effort, anti-struggle. Here is a life speaking the highest philosophy but involved in a profession which is apparently an unleashing of ego's energy. What are the issues? What are the contradictions? Lee's life is worthy of exploration by posterity.

Relevance to Anthropology

A school in anthropological thought is a style in martial arts. Schools condition; they distort perception. They prevent total understanding.

So deconditioning is needed. Schools should be taught. But more important is to teach freedom from them. A researcher should approach study of a culture with openness. This should be emphasized in anthropologist's training.

Is not this approach relevant to other disciplines also? Maybe. But this is more relevant in Anthropology. Anthropologist's training involves giving him 'culture shock' through the study of the remote, the exotic. It is for this reason that there is a lot of discussion in Anthropology on how to study culture, the possible prejudices, the limitations of our concepts etc.

Bruce Lee's solutions are worthy of reflection. Maybe we can call Bruce Lee's approach Buddhist approach to fieldwork.

Anyway, what would a Buddhist inquire in a distant culture? Is it only kinship, stratification, technology, distribution of food etc? Maybe not, he might study the nature of conditioning, role of thought, role of ambition etc. The topics of study could be different as well!

Questions to think about

1) What is meant by 'No Way as Way'?
2) Why was Bruce Lee against developing a style which was better than all the previous styles?
3) How can a fighter engaged in a combat be against ego-consciousness?
4) What can an anthropologist learn from Bruce Lee's philosophy?
5) Would Krishnamurti approve of Bruce Lee's application of his philosophy?

My Sources

The books I followed to write the first edition.

1. *Cultural Materialism – The Struggle for a Science of Culture* (1979) by Marvin Harris. Pages: 380

Whatever clarity I have about *Anthropological Thought* I owe it to this book. I found this book extremely fascinating. The author explains his theoretical orientation "Cultural Materialism" and goes about critically evaluating in a very convincing and forcible way some of the alternative strategies – sociobiology, dialectical materialism, structuralism, structural Marxism, psychological and cognitive idealism, eclecticism and obscurantism. Though only one or two chapters in this book are directly relevant, I found that reading the whole book helped me develop a clear perspective of the entire field. I can't overemphasise the influence this book had on me.

In writing on structuralism, new ethnography, phenomenological approach, this book is particularly useful.

2. *The Rise of Anthropological Theory* (1968) by Marvin Harris. Pages: 800

This authoritative account of anthropological theory has been my primary source of information. I have referred to it for almost all the topics I wrote in this book. Whenever I came across different books presenting conflicting versions of any point, I chose the version given in this book.

However, this book is written "to prove a point", that is to look at the history of anthropological theory in the light of his theoretical orientation – cultural materialism and convey to the reader the superiority of his orientation. Reading his *Cultural*

Materialism helped me understand *The Rise of Anthropological Theory* better.

3. *Images of Man – A History of Anthropological Thought* (1974) by Annamarie de Waal Malefijt. Pages: 350

I referred to this for almost all the topics. This is written in a simple language. Whenever I found *Rise of Anthropological Theory* difficult, I turned to this.

4. *Theories of Man and Culture* (1973) by Elvin Hatch. I referred to this for functionalism, neo-evolutionism and cultural ecology.

5. *Anthropology* by Ember and Ember. Though only one chapter is devoted to anthropological thought, I got the gist of the subject which helped me provide an outline for the whole book.

Sources for the second edition

6. *Visions of Culture: An Introduction to Anthropological Theories and Theorists* (Third edition, 2009) by Jerry D. Moore

7. *Anthropological Theory* (fourth edition, 2008) by R. Jon McGee and Richard L. Warms gives a collection of original articles with comments by the editors.

8. *A History of Anthropological Theory* (fourth edition, 2013)   by Paul A. Ericson & Liam D. Murphy.

Wikipedia, YouTube videos have also been useful.

What I have added in the second edition:

- Morgan: Evolution of family and government

- Malinowski: Diary written during his fieldwork

- Mead: Controversy over her first book

- L'evi Strauss: Irawati Karve on kinship in India

- Leslie White: Marxist influence

- Julian Steward: Marxism and environment

- Brief chapter on Marvin Harris

- Gordon Childe, Ralph Linton, Karl Polanyi

- Victor Turner, Clifford Geertz, Schneider

- Harold C. Conklin, Stephen A. Tyler

- Update on Carlos Castaneda

- Feyerabend, Bruce Lee

www.ingramcontent.com/pod-product-compliance
Lightning Source LLC
Chambersburg PA
CBHW051441250726
48655CB00001B/171